Funny, I Don't Remember Any Good Dope Days

Robert J. Durst

Dedication

This book is dedicated to the memories of those who have lost their lives to addiction and to the courage of those who continue to battle that dreaded demon.

May their families find comfort, may the Lord give them strength in their battles, and may all men and women of goodwill join forces to defeat this horrific plague.

Preface

After his retirement, the author and his wife, Sandra, moved to South Florida. While in Florida, Bob and Sandra, together with several others, founded a non-profit, Can We Help, to serve the homeless with meals, clothing, and personal articles.

Through a providential series of circumstances evolving from his work with Can We Help, Bob was given the opportunity to serve as a Volunteer Chaplain in the county jail.

As a Chaplain, he met regularly with the homeless men and eventually a number of female addicts in one-on-one, eye-to-eye conversations where there were "no holds barred."

He came to know the homeless and the addicted as strong, complex, and internally beautiful people. He learned firsthand, up close and personal, what it is like to be homeless and witnessed the horrible struggles of those in the iron-fisted grip of addiction.

Both the homeless and addicts are generally very guarded, are skilled liars, and are master manipulators. They do not readily share the truths about their lives. However, Bob was taken into their inner circle of trust. He was able to share their deepest regrets, fears, dashed hopes, and failed dreams. He prayed, he cried, he rejoiced, and he developed friendships that have lasted to the present.

For many, he ministered to them about how the shame of homelessness and addiction had stripped them of any self-esteem or semblance of normalcy.

For many, the desperation of homelessness and addiction had caused them to spiral into prostitution and a variety of crimes that were beyond even their own imaginations but were absolutely necessary for them to simply survive and feed their voracious appetites for drugs.

For most, their homelessness and addictions had deprived them of or ended any family relationships.

For some, it cost them their lives.

Bob began his journey with the homeless and addicted with stereotypical perceptions. But, he soon changed his perceptions and came to know each person as an individual… individuals who once had the same hopes and dreams as everyone else.

Unfortunately, however, untreated mental illness, abject poverty, and the lack of any real and effective support systems made an escape from their realities nothing more than a dream for most.

The tragedies of their lives recycled again and again with failed rehabilitations, relapses, and broken promises.

Family members recounted to him how a beloved family member's addiction had destroyed their family. They responded with grief and remorse when he called to tell them that their son or daughter had died from an overdose.

By putting a face on homelessness and addiction, Bob hopes that the "opioid epidemic" will become more than a sound bite on the evening news or a political football that is tossed from one party, one politician to another, with ample amounts of finger-pointing. Maybe it will be seen for what it is—currently the greatest social crisis and the leading cause of death for our young people.

With greater awareness and understanding, it is hoped that people of good will rise up and say collectively that "this has to stop." These are our sons and daughters, our brothers and sisters who are dying at the rate of well over 100,000 per year.

For those who are still struggling with addiction, it is hoped that this book will show you that our God is big enough and gracious enough to free you from your demons, just as He has for some of those whose stories are told in this book.

The Magnitude of the Problems

The *National Alliance to End Homelessness, 2022 Edition,* estimates that there are almost 600,000 homeless men, women, and families in the United States. They estimate that families with children make up about 30%—or 180,000—of that total.

Of that total, about half have access to some form of shelter, and the other half live with virtually no shelter in the streets, in the woods, on trains and subways, and in vehicles.

Some experts estimate that the actual number of people without their own homes may be double or triple the 600,000 estimate if those who are "couch surfing" (moving from house to house and sleeping on floors or couches), living in sheds or garages on the property of friends or relatives, or those who are undetected in the surveys are taken into consideration.

For several years the numbers seemed to be decreasing, but in the last two years, they have begun to increase at the rate of 2-3% per year.

Drugs and alcohol are often an integral part of a homeless person's life, and when the effects of the escalating drug crises are layered on top of the alarming homeless statistics, homelessness and addiction can be seen for what they are—a societal crisis of epic proportions.

It would be hard to find anyone who has not heard the term "opioid epidemic," but is the extent of that nightmare fully understood by most?

Opioids are defined by the National Institute on Drug Abuse as *illegal heroin, synthetic opioids such as fentanyl, and prescription pain relievers such as oxycodone, hydrocodone, codeine, and morphine.*

In 2019, it was estimated that there were 10.1 million Americans (approximately 1 out of every 35 people!) were addicted to or abusing opioids.[1]

The impact of addiction is far-reaching and extends not only to the addict but to their children, their spouses, their extended families, and virtually everyone with whom they have contact.

The financial impact of addiction on individuals and their families is impossible to quantify, but the impact has clearly reached unparalleled levels. The costs of rehabilitation, bail, lawyers, counseling, and medical care are impossible to quantify but are estimated to be in the hundreds of millions of dollars each year.

The costs of addiction are not limited to the addict and their families. They extend to society at large. Added costs are incurred by society at large for detox and treatment facilities within the penal system, added overhead to hospital emergency rooms for the treatment of thousands of overdoses each year, law enforcement costs of additional training, and the costs of Narcan and other emergency detox deterrent drugs.

As best as can be estimated, the overall opioid epidemic costs are $78.5 billion per year.

However, the real *cost* is the human carnage.

There are countless millions of people who are empty shells of

---

[1] "2019 National Survey on Drug Use and Health," Substance Abuse and Mental Health Services Administration, Rockville, Md. Pub. # PEP 20-07-01-001.

themselves wandering our streets, living under bridges, and struggling just to get their next fix.

The death toll from drugs has escalated exponentially. The CDC—National Center for Health Statistics—estimated that from 1999 to 2020, there have been 841,000 overdose deaths.

SHADAC (State Health Access Data Assistance Center) estimated that in 2022, deaths from overdoses would exceed 100,000 per year for the first time in history.

And what have we done to attempt to stem this tide?

Big Pharma has been the target of a number of legal actions. The State of Oklahoma pursued Johnson & Johnson in 2019 and successfully imposed a $572 million fine. Purdue Pharmaceutical was charged with the overproduction and distribution of prescription opioids and paid a $4.5 billion fine. In 2020, the Justice Department sued Walmart, charging them with filling *hundreds of thousands of illegal prescriptions.*

However, many of those efforts are merely "picking the low-hanging fruit." Those efforts do not address the drugs that are pouring into our country through drug cartels in Mexico and from the government of China.

The DEA's Heroin Signature Program, which endeavors to identify the source of opioids in America, has estimated that 92% of the heroin seized by law enforcement came from Mexico.

Within the last few years, our country's open or "relaxed" southern border policies have resulted in a dramatic increase in the flow of drugs from Mexico into the United States.

In 2021, fentanyl—the newest opioid threat—became the

leading cause of overdose deaths.[2]

Fentanyl is a synthetic opioid. It is 50-100 times more powerful than morphine and is prized by drug dealers because of its strength and corresponding ability to *hook* users after only one or two uses.

It is coveted by addicts to give them a high because their extended use of heroin has eliminated its ability to do so without some additives.

It is, however, deadly, and just a few small grains of it can bring instant death.

As with heroin, Mexico has been identified as the primary source of fentanyl imported into the United States.[3]

> "...chemicals used to make fentanyl are produced in China and shipped to clandestine labs in Mexico. Drug cartels are smuggling massive amounts of fentanyl across the Southwest border."

The chemical components used in Mexico to manufacture fentanyl usually come from China.

Mexican drug cartels are estimated to be making billions of dollars per year transporting and selling heroin and fentanyl into the United States while we sit back and watch the number of heroin and fentanyl overdose deaths escalate dramatically.

---

[2] DEA, "Fentanyl 2021."

[3] "Fentanyl Flow to the United States" DEA Intelligence Report, DEA-DCT-DIR-008-20-1/20.

Contents

Chapter 1
AN ENDING and A BEGINNING

The room was emptying. The stragglers were saying good night to each other, and several others had gone to the bar for a nightcap. I was gathering up the cards, well-wishes, and a new set of golf clubs.

The retirement party given to me by my partners was heartfelt. My family had been invited, and their presence made the evening even more special. The fact that it was held at the Trenton Country Club, where I had served as President for the past six years, made it even more meaningful.

After forty-three years of practicing law, I decided to retire and enjoy a life of leisure. As I sat through the good-natured roasting and old *war stories,* I wondered what retirement would be like. I had worked since I was a teenager and eagerly anticipated life in South Florida, on the beach, with time to play golf and tennis and to travel with my wife, Sandra.

The room was almost empty. The Managing Partner at the law firm, Lew, came over and sat down beside me.

"We are really going to miss you," Lew said as he put an arm of friendship on my shoulder. But no one believes that you are really going to retire. We are going to keep your office for you just in case you change your mind."

"Lew, this firm has been my life for almost half a century, and I couldn't ask for better partners, but I am really retiring. So, if you ever want to see lights on in that office again, you are going to have to hire someone else to turn them on and off. Sandra and I have worked hard, and it is time for us to take some time for ourselves.

1

But I do appreciate your offer."

"Talk him into staying," said one of the servers who was clearing the tables, "and then maybe we can get him to continue as President here at the club."

"Kathy, you know that I love this place, but after six years, it is time for a change."

"We're heading down to "God's Waiting Room," as some call it, and put our feet up. I will miss all of you, and I could not have survived six years as President of this club without a great staff. I'll be back up from time to time, and I don't ever want to come here for dinner unless you are our server."

I had just turned 66, and Sandra and I had purchased a home on Sand Island just off Seaside Beach in Southeast Florida, where we had been snowbirding for the past few years.

"You know, Lew, we have been through a lot together. We both have helped to build this firm into something that will be here long after we both are gone. Now it's time to let the young'uns take it over. They don't need a bunch of old guys hanging around taking up office space. The last thing I ever want to do is anything that will hurt the firm, and having an old guy hanging around in a corner office isn't a good business model."

"What are you going to do to keep yourself from going crazy down there? You aren't going to be content by just sitting on the beach and playing golf."

"Watch me," I replied. "And if you can ever pull yourself away from this place, you and that good wife of yours have an open invitation to come visit."

We embraced, and Sandra and I drove off into the night for one of our last rides home from the Trenton Country Club.

The house had been sold, excess furniture was sold or given away, and we were leaving for Florida by the end of the week.

"Do you think you can really retire?" Sandra asked.

"Honey, I don't know, and to be honest, it frightens me a little. But let's just play it by ear and see where life takes us."

Chapter 2
A DARK and DREARY NIGHT

Sandra and I had been in Florida for about two years, and despite my intentions of not working, we both were "working" almost full-time.

We had founded a non-profit corporation, Can We Help, and I had just finished an unusually busy day at the Can We Help offices in downtown Seaside Beach.

Instead of spending my days on the beach or golf course, we committed ourselves to helping the homeless in Seaside Beach. Our days were filled with arranging meals for homeless men and women, collecting clothing and toiletries to distribute to them, and then finding donors, grants, funds, or resource partners to make it all possible.

As an additional part of my responsibility to Can We Help, I served as a Volunteer Chaplain to the homeless who found themselves incarcerated in the Anderson County Jail. Recently, the jail visits had expanded from just homeless men to include a growing number of young female heroin addicts.

As was often the case, I had not been able to see all of the inmates that I had scheduled to visit that day and had decided to go back that evening to see those that I had been unable to see during my daytime visits.

I am not a patient person, and the tedium of that particular day had not put me in an upbeat frame of mind when I was finally able to leave the office.

As I drove home, the temperatures were falling, and there was an unusually cold drizzle of rain. The night was moonless, and the stars were hidden by the cloudy skies.

Yes, even in South Florida, there can be cold spells.

The cold spells were not good for the homeless men and women who had to suffer through them in the woods with no heat, no electricity, and shelters that barely kept them dry, much less warm.

"What a day! Nancy and I were swamped in the jail, and I had to leave without seeing some of the ladies who I think really need a visit," I mumbled as I sat down in my recliner.

Sandra was finishing the preparation of our evening meal and urged me to just stay home. "It's not a night to go back out. Just sit and get some rest."

"It's not a night I want to go back out, but I really have to go back to the jail to see a couple of the ladies. You know how it is… maybe a real crisis, maybe just a way to get out of their cell and have an hour or so and to talk with someone other than the ladies on the cell block, who knows?"

"Sit down, enjoy your meal, catch your breath, and if you have to go back out, at least relax for an hour or so," Sandra suggested.

As always, good advice. And after an hour or so of rest and one of Sandra's wonderful meals, I headed back to the jail. As I came out of the house and drove down the street, I realized it was dark, very dark. The darkness and the cold mist of rain seemed like the opening scene of an old vampire movie.

I drove down the street and turned toward the gate leading out of the community. As I approached the guard house, I stopped to

5

shout a greeting to the officers on duty.

"Where are you going on a night like this?" one of the officers asked.

"I'm going to jail... they finally caught up with me!"

As I drove across town, I had an uneasy feeling. I had been to the Anderson County Jail numerous times, but tonight it felt different. I had an unsettled feeling and confusion about the ladies I was going to see and what I would say to them that evening. Nancy, who was rapidly becoming a full-fledged Chaplain herself, was not available to go with me this evening, and I missed her.

The streetlights were eerie, with halos of mist around each light, and the streets were about empty of traffic.

South Florida people just don't go out on nights like this.

Chapter 3
THE DRIVE

I came out of the community and turned right onto A1A, then made the left onto Indian Street and headed across town to the jail.

"Damn! On a night like this, I don't need to sit here and watch a train roll by for fifteen minutes," I exclaimed. But that was exactly what I was going to have to do. The red lights were flashing, and the bell was ringing. The gates came down, and I could hear the train's horn announcing its arrival. Most trains this time of night were very long freight trains carrying car after car of gravel up from the Keys. The trains were usually about 2 miles long and took ten to fifteen minutes to clear the crossing.

Oh well. Put the car in park and sit back.

Feeling a bit sorry for myself, I glanced over to my left, and my thoughts drifted to the fifteen or so homeless men and women I knew lived in those woods behind the Indian Street strip mall.

Why am I feeling sorry for myself? Think about those folks on an evening like this.

After what seemed like an extraordinarily long time, the last car of gravel passed, the bell rang, and the gates went up. I proceeded on Indian Street and almost missed the turn into the jail as my mind continued to ponder the plight of the homeless on such a dank and cold night.

As I turned into the jail, I noticed for the first time that the long, winding driveway from the highway into the jail had no street lights.

That's weird. You would think they would want the only road into and out of jail to be well-lit.

I parked the car and put up an umbrella for the walk from the parking lot up to the entrance to the jail. As I approached the building, the building itself seemed particularly gloomy. Shrouded in mist with slivers of light coming through its small narrow, horizontal windows, I thought the building looked like a monster staring out into the dark evening through slit-like eyes.

As I walked into the empty visitors' waiting room, the TV mounted high on one of the walls displayed a "talking head" babbling on about something, and the rose-colored plastic chairs looked cold and uninviting.

A Trustee prisoner was emptying trash and cleaning up after the day's visitors.

"Hey, Eugene, are they paying you overtime to work tonight?" I teased the Trustee.

Officer Jane was the Sheriff's officer on duty behind the thick glass window where all visitors were required to check-in. I walked over to the window and leaned down to speak through the small, shiny metal opening in the glass. The thick glass window and the small metal opening reminded me of the movie theater I went to as a kid.

"Chaplain Bob, what are you doing here on a night like this?" Jane asked.

"Just here for a date with two of my favorite ladies on a beautiful South Florida evening," I responded.

If you think this is a nice Florida evening, maybe you are the one who needs some counseling, Chaplain," Jane parried back.

"Who are you here to see? And please tell me that you won't be roaming all around tonight. You know how the officers are about bringing inmates up for visits after they have fed and secured them for the evening."

Fed and secured them for the evening. I knew exactly what Jane meant, but somehow those words seemed odd this evening. *Sounds like a horse stable,* I thought. *All fed and secured.*

"No, just some easy work tonight, Jane. Both ladies are in Pod 2, so I won't be of much trouble to the officers."

"Okay, let me call and see what's going on up there. Take a load off your feet and sit down for a few minutes."

I had learned that if you were going to encounter any difficulty with a jail visit, it was usually on the evening shift. Most night shift officers were working two jobs and had put in a full day's work before coming on duty. They were good, hard-working people, but they weren't inclined to do any heavy lifting after the inmates were all "fed and secured," so I didn't know how long it would take or what to expect from upstairs.

In a few minutes, Jane came into the waiting room with her wand in hand. "Let me scan you. And you're in luck… the meal is done, cleaned up, and neither of your ladies has shower time tonight, so they are up there waiting for you."

After she had waved her metal detecting wand up and down my body and leafed through my Bible, she said, "You're clear except for that buzzing in your pocket. If those are car keys, leave them with me. Only one pencil or pen… and I need to see it on your way out. Don't give anything to the ladies. If you want to leave anything with them, give it to the officer to inspect and let

9

them give it to the inmate. No touching, no hugging, no handshakes. You know the drill. Just stick to it and have a good evening with your dates."

I had heard the rules dozens of times and understood that they were absolutely necessary in a place that is occupied by people who, by definition, are rule breakers. Inmates are masters at circumventing rules and using every circumvention to their advantage.

"Thanks, Jane, and see you on the way down."

"You better," she replied, "I've got your car keys!"

With that, Jane pushed the buzzer, and the door that led from the waiting room into the jail itself popped open.

"Close it behind you," she told me.

Chapter 4
THE LONG HALLWAY and THE WAIT

No matter how many times I had entered through the door from the visitors' waiting room into the jail, the sound of that heavy metal door closing behind me and the click of the lock sliding into place always gave me a shiver. I was now in their territory, and I knew that I could only get back out if someone opened that door for me.

Every step I took was now on video cameras. I was often tempted to dance or wave, but I knew that I was in their territory, and they may not think my antics were as humorous as I intended.

I pushed the button to open the elevator door, stepped inside, and pressed the '2' button. The old elevator bumped and rattled a bit but got me safely to the second floor.

As I stepped out into the hallway, I experienced intense silence. No one was in sight, not a sound to be heard.

What a difference from the daytime hustle and bustle.

During the day, the hallways were a beehive of activity with attorneys scurrying to see their clients, GED teachers going back and forth to their classrooms, 12-Step Program presenters scurrying to their classrooms, and officers escorting prisoners to the calls of "prisoner coming through," which required that anyone other than the officer escorting a prisoner had to step aside, stand still, and allow the officer and prisoner to pass.

That night, the hallway was completely empty and quiet.

The ever-present smells of a jail seemed particularly strong. The smells of cleaning fluids, an unidentifiable smell wending its way up from the kitchen, and the smell of simply too many humans in a confined space.

And on a rainy night, there were ever-present towels under virtually every metal framed window. *Why do these windows leak so much, and why don't they fix them?* They always seemed to leak no matter how much or how little it was raining.

On the floor under each narrow slit of a window, there were towels lying on the floor. Towels that absorbed the water running down the walls under the windows. *Does anyone ever wash those towels? In fact, does anyone ever even dry those towels?* I wondered as a distinct odor of mildew reached my nostrils.

As I walked down the hallway, every step echoed. Tonight, the hallway seemed exceptionally long, but soon I was at the door to Pod 2. I pushed the buzzer and waited for someone to answer on the scratchy speaker.

The answer was always the same: "Yes, who is it, and what is your business?"

What a dumb question. I am the only one here tonight. Jane has not only told them that I was coming, but they have been watching me on their monitors.

"Chaplain Bob to see Danielle and Ashlee," I responded.

Buzz, click, the door opened, and I proceeded down several steps into the small room furnished with metal tables with attached plastic seats. I selected one of the three tables and laid my Bible and notebook down.

The speaker beside the door crackled out: "Who do you want first, Chaplain?"

"Up to you, whoever is free and ready to come up," I replied.

In a few minutes, the speaker garbled out another message: "Gonna take a little while. We have an incident to take care of right now. Give us fifteen to twenty minutes." Click. The speaker clicked off.

An "incident" could mean one of many things—an inmate was having a meltdown, a fight had broken out, someone was having a medical problem, or any one of countless other matters that required a lockdown in the cell block. No matter what it was, it always meant the same thing—sit down and wait... we'll bring them up when we are ready. There was no deviation. No way to hurry it up. No way to do anything but wait.

It may take a while, so I sat back and listened to the rain. *It was sure raining a lot harder now*, I thought as I listened to the rain hitting the skylight and metal roof. I waited for the speaker to bark out again.

Chapter 5
I PONDER

Jane's words continued to run through my mind as I sat waiting—*fed and secured.*

I couldn't stop thinking about the impact of those words.

How dehumanizing. But this is a place that dehumanizes people.

Orange jumpsuits that seldom fit properly, shower sandals for shoes, eat on schedule, shower on schedule, and have no ability to personalize your life other than a few pictures in your cell or maybe a few books.

As those thoughts ran through my mind, I thought of the two women I was about to meet. I was really very fond of them both. They were both badly damaged individuals. But they were just that… individuals… strong and intelligent individuals who had seemingly been dealt a very "bad hand" in the game of life.

Individuals who had hopes, dreams, fears, and feelings.

They weren't just numbers. They were people. Real people. People who had stumbled and fallen but were trying to get up and move forward.

Have they been fed and secured?

Will they be dressed in those baggy orange jumpsuits and shower sandals?

Within the penal system, addicts and homeless are often taken for granted and are viewed with more than a slight degree of disrespect.

But I didn't disrespect these ladies. I had grown to know and like both of them. I knew them as people—as individuals. I knew the paths they had traveled to get here. I knew the wars that were raging within them.

But what does the outside world think of a person—particularly a young woman—after they have worn those orange jumpsuits and were locked in a cage? A cage, isn't that a little harsh? I don't think so, I thought.

A cage that was literally the edifice of bricks and steel that I was sitting in and a psychological cage created by childhood abuse, sexual abuse, domestic violence, simply bad decisions, or plain old bad luck.

Maya Angelou addressed it when she wrote **I Know Why the Caged Bird Sings.**

I loved Ms. Angelou's quotation: "Do the best you can until you know better. Then when you know better, do better."

Am I helping these women to 'know better' and then 'do better'?

All of the women I visited were once little girls. Many had been the apples of their parents' eyes… the hopes and dreams of their parents. They were daughters, sisters, and even mothers.

They once played with dolls or kicked soccer balls, took dance lessons, or played instruments and sang. Now they filled their days reading well-worn paper-bound books and playing cards with decks of cards that seldom had all fifty-two cards while sitting in their cage.

They were allowed out of their cells and into the common areas at strictly regulated times.

They were allowed an every-other-day shower under video observation.

They ate their meals on strict schedules and en masse.

They found corners that were out of range of the omnipresent cameras to steal a kiss or a hug from a new girlfriend.

Some once had aspirations of going to college and dreams of careers. Now, most had now been expelled from high school and were struggling through GED classes to get their high school diploma. Their only career dreams now were a hope that someone, anyone, would hire a "junkie" when they got out.

How have their lives gone so terribly wrong that they are now simply an 'addict,' an 'inmate,' a 'whore'? And why are they living in a 'cage'?

The friends and relatives who had come to their birthday parties, their sporting events, their dance recitals, their graduations, and even their weddings had given up and were now nowhere to be found. Families had been shattered by failed efforts and the frustrations of dealing with an addicted child.

Some even had their own children who had disappeared down the rabbit hole of the foster system.

Grandparents had closed their doors after they had been the victims of the addict's thefts.

Sanctimonious spouses who may have themselves been a large part of the addicts' use of drugs had turned their heads, blaming all of their own failures on her and her drugs.

The carnage of addiction was vast and deep.

Am I, Bob, equipped to wade through all of this and be of any help?

I had no training as an addiction counselor. I probably couldn't name three of the twelve steps to recovery. I had never been an addict, and thankfully, no one in my immediate family was an addict. I had never even raised a daughter; I had two sons.

Am I capable of helping these 'Caged Birds' sing?

My thoughts were suddenly interrupted when the scratchy speaker blurted out: "You ready, Chaplain? The first one is coming your way."

Chapter 6
MY ARGUMENT WITH GOD

In a few minutes, Ashlee came into the room with a huge smile and gave me an enthusiastic air hug.

Ashlee was a charmer, and her years on the streets had given her people skills far beyond her youthful appearance. She was a very attractive, athletic-looking young woman, but the rigors of addiction and street life were beginning to take their toll on her. She was a hard-core heroin addict who had grown up in a dysfunctional family with some family members who were also addicts. She was now struggling mightily to overcome her addiction, but unfortunately, this was not her first rodeo. She had been through several cycles of sobriety and relapse.

She had become a fairly regular guest of the county, finding her way into the county jail once or twice a year for a litany of minor offenses.

"I missed you today and am so glad you are here. I've been reading my Bible about the things we discussed the last time, and I can't wait to discuss some of them with you."

"Do you really believe God knew me before I was even born?" she asked.

"With all my heart, I believe that, Ashlee. Let's look at Jeremiah 1:5, Isaiah 49:1, and Romans 8:29."

We read together the teachings that God knew us before he formed us in the womb, that God called us from the womb and gave us our names, and that God had formed us in the image of his own son while we were yet in the womb.

"Does he still know me and love me after all that I have done?" Ashlee asked.

"He sure does, and he is waiting to welcome you back. Do you remember the story about the prodigal son we read the last time?"

"Yes, and that's what I want to talk about. What I can't get my head around is that if I can't forgive myself, how can I expect God and other people to forgive me?" she asked.

"I have a beautiful daughter that I may have put at risk. How can I forgive myself, and how can God forgive me for that?"

"Ashlee, what you have done and where your life has taken you is not you, and it is not of God. It is Satan, plain and simple. Satan has whispered his lies in your ear for years, and you have believed him."

"Satan! Do you really believe that there is a Satan... a little man running around with horns and a pitchfork?"

"Yep. I don't know if that is what he looks like, but I sure do, and I know that he tries to whisper in my ear almost every day."

"Do you remember when we read about Jesus going out into the desert to be tempted by Satan before he began his ministry? If Satan is not real, then that whole story about Jesus' temptations would be meaningless, wouldn't it?" I rhetorically asked Ashlee.

"Let's read something that Paul wrote in Chapter 7 of Romans... and you tell me if it has any meaning to you.

"St. Paul, the great St. Paul, tells us that he had a steadfast desire to do what was good, but he could not do it. He admits that he couldn't stop doing things that he did not want to be doing.

19

"He tells us that it is not even him who is doing or not doing those things. It is the evil that is living within him. That evil that St. Paul was struggling with is what I believe to be Satan."

"You also tell us about demons. Is Satan the same as the demons you talk about?" she asked.

"Yes and no, the Bible tells us that Jesus cast demons out of people. We don't really know what those demons were. They could have been drugs, they could have been a mental illness, or they could have been an actual demon."

"But yes, Ashlee, I believe when scripture tells us that Jesus cast out demons, he was using peoples' faith to remove whatever evil they had allowed Satan to put into their lives."

Ashlee said that she had read about the woman who fought through the crowd, crawled on the ground, and reached out to touch the hem of Jesus' robe. The woman was immediately freed of her demons, and Jesus told her that her faith had healed her.

"Do you believe that, Chaplain Bob?" she asked. "Do you believe that Jesus will cast out our demons just because we have faith in him?"

"You bet I do, and I know it is true because I have my own demons, and I know that it is only when I put my faith in Jesus that I can be free of them," I replied.

"Do you think I have demons?" Ashlee asked.

Wow! On this dark and drizzly night, it seemed that Ashlee was on the verge of a breakthrough. I was sure glad that I hadn't let Satan whisper in my ear to stay home instead of coming out to share this evening with Ashlee.

"Ashlee, you most certainly have your own 'demon.' Your 'demon' seems to be much like St. Paul's demon.

"I want you to take my Bible right now and read again what Paul wrote about not being able to do what he knew was right and not being able to stop doing what he knew was wrong. See whether Paul is just telling us about himself or is he telling you about yourself.

"Do you want to end your addiction but can't? Do you hate doing drugs, but you can't stop?"

As Ashlee was reading, I drifted off into my own thoughts, and the unsettled feeling I had earlier in the evening began to overtake me.

When Ashlee finished reading, she looked at me and asked, "Mr. Bob, where are you? You look worried tonight."

Surprised that my feelings were showing, I replied, "I am. In fact, I am just having a little argument."

"An argument, with who?" Ashlee asked. "There is no one else here besides you and me."

"I'm having an argument with God."

"Wait just a fucking minute. You are arguing with God! What's that all about? I thought you guys were on the same team!"

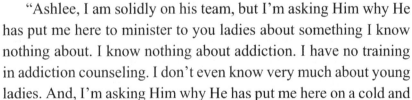
"Ashlee, I am solidly on his team, but I'm asking Him why He has put me here to minister to you ladies about something I know nothing about. I know nothing about addiction. I have no training in addiction counseling. I don't even know very much about young ladies. And, I'm asking Him why He has put me here on a cold and rainy night trying to do something that I don't feel I am capable of

21

doing. I'm trying to tell Him that I don't belong here and asking Him to just let me get back to feeding and helping homeless people," I answered.

"Whoa, you're telling me not to let Satan whisper in my ear, and it sounds like you are letting him shout in your face!" Ashlee said. "You just don't get it, do you, Mr. Bob?"

"I guess not, or I wouldn't be having this argument with God."

"Let me tell you why you are here," Ashlee said as she pulled herself up straight and looked me directly in the eyes. "You never fail us. If you tell us you will be here, you're here. We're not used to people keeping their promises, and it means a lot when someone does. You don't tell us what to do. We have plenty of people telling us what to do; go to rehab, go to NA, do the 12 Steps, get a job. Like they know what's best for us. Most of us have done that shit for years, and it hasn't gotten us out of this mess. What the hell do they know about what we're going through and what we need?

But you… you are different. You don't try to tell us what to do. In fact, you tell us not to listen to you. You tell us to go find the answers ourselves—in the Bible and in prayer. You show us that with God's help, we can get ourselves out of this mess. That's why you are here. Got it?"

Ashlee went on, "Just like tonight, you just told me to read this Chapter again and to think about what it is saying. You didn't try to tell me what it was saying or what I should do with it."

"Sometimes when I go back down there and reread these things you give us to read, I laugh out loud 'cause I find just the answer I need.

The fact is, none of us are going to find God on our own. Most of us don't even know where to look. That's what you are here for. Now you stop your dumbass argument, get yourself home, get some rest, and I'll keep reading and praying until we can talk again on Thursday."

I gave Ashlee a big air hug and ended the session, giving thanks for her and her words of wisdom.

Totally forgetting that I was to see Danielle. I left the conference room and began that long walk back down the hallway. This time I didn't hear the echoes, see the shiny walls or even notice the towels on the floor.

My favorite hymns were running through my mind, and all I could think of was how privileged I was to have people like Ashlee in my life.

No more arguments, Lord. If this is where you want me, I'm in.

23

Chapter 7
OOPS, FORGOT SOMEONE

As I left the jail and was driving home through the cold drizzle, my mind was still swirling about Ashlee's comments and the unlikely road I had traveled to now be ministering to these wonderful ladies.

Damn!! Do I ever come across this railroad crossing when there isn't a train coming?

I brought the car to a stop in a line of traffic, waiting for the train to pass. As I sat there listening to the seemingly endless rumble of the gravel-laden freight cars passing by, it hit me like a lightning bolt.

I forgot to see Danielle! Oh my God, I had two ladies to see, and I totally forgot one of them!

I had been so focused on Ashlee and what she had said to me that I left without seeing Danielle.

I glanced at my watch and thought, *there is still time to go back and see her before lights out. Should I turn around and go back?*

I pulled out of line and did a U-turn. As the horns behind me blared and drivers cursed, I headed back to the jail.

"What's up with you, Chaplain? Did your wife not let you back into the house, and you need to stay here for the evening?" Officer Jane said to me as I hurried up to the window and handed her my driver's license and keys.

"Nah, I just got distracted and forgot to see one of the ladies. Can you call up there and see if it is okay for me to come and see

Danielle?"

"You are not going to make friends with the officers up there. She'll still be here in the morning. Why don't you go home and come back tomorrow?"

"I can't, Jane. I promised her I would see her tonight, and I have to keep that promise."

"Okay, okay… I'll check."

"They said to come on up, although they didn't sound too happy about it."

"They'll get over it. They have the rest of the night to play on their phones and gossip. I'll only be a little while."

Danielle was in her early twenties, maybe 23-24, but she had been through several years of heavy heroin usage. She had told me that she had a very normal and happy childhood until a boyfriend tore his rotator cuff and was given OxyContin for the pain. For some reason, she experimented with Oxy, and within a year, she was addicted.

Over the past few years, she had been in and out of the county jail several times and may be facing her first stint in state prison for something that she refused to talk about.

At this point, she wasn't using heroin just to get high. She was using it because she needed it. Without it, she would become deathly sick—dope sick.

I learned about "dope sick" from observing several addicts going through it. It was horrendous! Chills, shakes, cramps, and, in some instances, life-threatening impacts on a person's heart and lungs.

Danielle got her supply of pills by going from pain clinic to pain clinic where she could gather up prescriptions for as many as 150 pills a month. Simple… easy, peasy.

Wait in line with about a dozen others and then out the door with a prescription and a $75 charge, always payable in cash only, for a "pain analysis" with a doctor whom she had never met or seen.

One day when she was really dope sick and out of funds, a girlfriend introduced her to a new way to get her dope money. The girlfriend drove her to a man's house, and after forty minutes of sex, she left with over $200, from which the girlfriend took $75.

The depth of her addiction and the fear of dope sickness made her forget who she was and led her to do things that she would not otherwise have even considered.

But, what a great way to keep herself supplied. She was soon turning tricks every day to get the money she needed to prevent herself from going into that horrible dope sickness.

This time she had been in jail for about three months and was completely detoxed. She was vowing not to go back to her life of dope and prostitution.

Maybe, just maybe, this was the time that she would actually get her life back under control.

Over the past several weeks, Danielle was more anxious than ever before to pray and read scripture.

I hoped that in a few more weeks, she might be released, turn the corner, and begin to recover from several chaotic and destructive years.

After the elevator, the long hallway, and the buzzers, Danielle came into the room with a huge smile on her face.

"I'm so glad you came back. I just wanted to tell you that I am getting out of here tomorrow morning,"

"Danielle, you are making such great progress, but I'm not sure that you are ready to go back out there just yet."

Danielle went into a long litany, which I had heard several times before, that she had a good job, this time working for a guy installing tile flooring. She was going to live with a sober friend, and they were hooked up with a great church.

Yea, yea, I had heard it all before and feared that it would have as little staying power as it had the last several times. But I had no way to dissuade Danielle, and even if I could, it was doubtful that the jail wanted to keep her any longer.

What could I say?

"Well, those are some big challenges. I wish you the very, very best, and please let me know if you need anything. You have my cell phone number."

As I walked down the long hallway to leave the jail, I prayed that it would work for Danielle this time, but I feared that the next time I would hear from her was when she was back in jail or worse.

Chapter 8

HOW IT ALL BEGAN

This had been an emotional night with Ashlee and Danielle. As I walked back down the hallway to the elevator, this time, it was Danielle that was on my mind.

Who is this new employer? Who is the friend? Can she stay away from Oxy and heroin?

Ashlee's words came back to my mind. "You don't tell us what to do. You tell us to try to find the answers for ourselves in the Bible and in prayer."

Listen to what Ashlee told you. You are not in control here, so don't tell Danielle what to do.

I reached the elevator and pushed the button to go back down to the lobby. The elevator came to its usual shuddering halt on the ground floor, and I pushed the buzzer for Jane to open the door and allow me to exit into the waiting room.

"Good night, Jane, and thanks for your help this evening," I called as I walked through the waiting room and was about to exit the jail.

"Aren't you forgetting something, Chaplain?" Jane called back. "You are not going to get far without your car keys."

"Thanks, Jane. I'm sorry my mind was wandering."

As I walked across the almost empty parking lot to my car, I then began reminiscing about how all this had begun.

How did all this evolve? How did I go from the evening of my retirement party at the Trenton Country Club to this?

28

It had been a circuitous route, but somehow, and for some reason, this seemed to be where God wanted me to be, and Ashlee's words seemed to confirm that. But I still wasn't convinced.

As I drove home, I thought about another cold evening several years earlier.

That's when it all began.

Sandra and I, along with two other couples, had spent the evening at a fine steakhouse in Seaside Beach celebrating a birthday. We all lived on the barrier island, Sand Island, across the Intracoastal Waterway from Seaside Beach and had to cross the causeway and bridge over the Indian River Lagoon to get home.

As we were driving onto the bridge, something caught my eye.

"Wait a minute, what's that down there on the boat ramp? I see fire. Maybe we better check it out."

We turned onto the ramp leading down to the picnic and boat launch area under the bridge to investigate.

As we drew closer, we were able to see a huddled group of men and women standing around a metal trash can in which there was a roaring fire.

"Is everything okay?" I called out the passenger window.

"Naw, nothing wrong," a raspy, gruff voice barked back. "We're just trying to stay warm on a cold night."

"Okay, have a good evening."

Others in the car explained that this was a group of homeless men and women who congregated under the bridge most evenings.

Some lived on the several derelict boats moored in the area, some walked to the bridge from the woods along the railroad tracks in Seaside Beach, and others slept on the benches under the bridge.

As we drove back up the ramp, I wondered why I had just wished a group of homeless folks huddled around a fire in a trash can a "good evening."

How can they be having a good evening by anyone's definition of what a good evening should be?

I broke the silence in the car, "Hey, guys, I bet those folks would welcome a good hot meal. Let's go home and try to pull something together for them."

As soon as we got home, the whole group pitched in to begin heating up some spaghetti sauce, boiling pasta, and heating up some frozen loaves of French bread that someone had pulled out of their freezer.

Within the hour, we headed back up the island and down the ramp with a large pot of spaghetti and a couple of loaves of French bread.

"Could you guys use a warm pot of spaghetti and some hot bread?"

Almost in unison, the immediate response was, "You bet!"

The next day the spaghetti meal was the talk of the small condo community where we lived. Our neighbors began offering thoughts and suggestions. "How hard would it be to take those folks a meal once a week?"

"I don't know how often they are there, but I will go up and try to find out," I offered.

The next evening I went back up to the area. Sure enough, essentially, the same group was there.

"Hi, I'm the guy who brought the spaghetti last night."

"We know who you are. And man-oh-man, was that meal great!"

They told me that the picnic area under the bridge was a safe gathering place for them. The police would not bother them if they stayed in the picnic area and didn't do any damage.

"So, how about another meal next Thursday?" I asked the group.

"Are you serious? Why would you bring another meal to us?"

"Because we want to and because we enjoyed talking with you guys."

"You are not going to get us to turn down a good meal. Thanks, we'll see you next Thursday."

As I drove away, I could see the looks on their faces—*yea, sure, bet we never see this guy again.*

I had been volunteering a day a week at a local food pantry. Each day homeless men and women would come to the pantry for their day bags, which contained enough non-perishable food for an evening meal.

The next day I struck up a conversation with one of the regulars, Jerry, who came in just about every day for a day bag. I told him about the meal we were going to do next Thursday under the Seaside Beach Causeway bridge.

"Why don't you guys come up?"

And, just how do you expect us to get there? It's a 5-mile walk, and none of us are going to ride our bikes in the dark."

Jerry lived in the woods behind the day labor hall on Indian Street and said he thought he could get the hall to allow us to serve meals in the parking area behind the building if I would put my money where my mouth was and actually bring a meal to them.

"Let me think about that and see if we have enough volunteers to serve meals at two locations—up under the bridge and down here. I'll get back to you," I replied.

Sandra was concerned that we could not cook two meals a week in our home but came up with an ingenious way to get the two meals a week that we would need. She made a list of friends, fellow golf club members, and church friends and asked each person to commit to making just one meal a year. The response was overwhelming, and we soon had a waiting list of people who wanted to provide their one meal per year.

With a group of steadfast volunteers and with Sandra and her friends Lynne and Donna going to pick up the meals, we soon had a well-oiled machine that was easily providing two hot, home-cooked meals per week to the homeless both under the bridge to Sand Island and five miles away in South Seaside Beach.

Within a few months, the number of meals and volunteers expanded to the point that it was necessary to organize and formalize the efforts. The group formed a not-for-profit corporation for which Lynne suggested the name Can We Help.

Little did I expect that this newly formed Can We Help would eventually lead me to become a Volunteer Chaplain in the Anderson County Jail.

Chapter 9
ALL I SEE IS ORANGE, and I CAN'T HEAR YOU

Over the next several months, Jerry and I forged a friendship, and Jerry became my liaison to the homeless.

Generally, homeless people are very, very suspicious of strangers for a variety of reasons. Some have open warrants for their arrest. Some suffer from mental illnesses that inhibit them from interacting with strangers. Some have simply dropped out and don't want to be found.

Every homeless person also has to protect their belongings. Everything they own is kept at their camps, and they are very careful about who has access to or even knows the location of their camps.

Jerry was well known to most of the homeless, and those that knew him trusted him. Through Jerry, I was able to connect with most of the homeless in the Seaside Beach area, and with Jerry's endorsement, I had access to their camps—a rare privilege for an outsider.

The ability to walk through the woods, enter various camps, ask questions, and get reliable answers was invaluable.

I was often asked by local law enforcement to help them locate someone living in the woods or on the street.

I would always do so, but with the unwritten understanding that unless it was an extremely unusual or emergent situation, I would not help them find and arrest any homeless person.

I would help them respond to the calls that would come to the Sheriff's office or the local police saying that a long-lost family

33

member was thought to be living somewhere in the woods in the Seaside Beach area and asking if someone could relay a message to them about a family illness or death. I would help Social Security, the VA, or Volunteers in Medicine find clients and patients to relay information or schedule appointments. Even the school district would occasionally have to contact parents or a homeless student.

Homeless people don't have listed telephone numbers, and they don't get mail deliveries. Some had cell phones, but the batteries were often dead. But, with Jerry's assistance, he and I could locate and communicate with almost anyone in the woods.

I had never suspected Jerry of using any drugs. Jerry loved beer and drank plenty of it, but he always denied using any drugs.

Jerry worked almost every day as a day laborer out of the labor hall, where we had begun serving meals. His camp was about a hundred yards back into the woods behind the labor hall.

It was a substantial camp made of scavenged lumber, sheets of plywood, and several blue tarps. There was a small three-legged table that had a corner with a missing leg nailed to a tree. There were two chairs where Jerry and I often spent an evening solving the world's problems. There were two mattresses inside the shelter, each resting on platforms also made of scavenged lumber. Outside the shelter, there was a fire pit with an iron grate across it and an old coffee pot usually filled with hot coffee at any hour of the day or night. There was an old two-by-four nailed between two trees that carried an impressive variety of cooking utensils. Jerry prided himself in always cooking an evening meal with the day bag he was able to pick up from the food pantry just across A1A.

Jerry's home reminded me of some of the *forts and shacks* my friends and I had built in the woods as kids, but this was not a child's play shack. It was a home... Jerry's home, and he took great pride in it.

Jerry did have a cell phone and a screw-in plug, which he would take to one of the light fixtures at the rear doors of the labor hall, unscrew the light bulb, insert a screw-in plug into the socket, and plug in his cell for charging.

I began to get suspicious that something was going on in Jerry's camp. Jerry had begun to change from welcoming me into his camp to being somewhat reluctant to allow me to come to his camp.

What's going on with Jerry?

One Thursday night, at the labor hall meal, I got the answer. It was a surprising answer. Jerry had been arrested and charged with both possession and sale of drugs—heroin.

Several of the other homeless men approached me and asked if I would go to the jail to visit Jerry.

"Jerry puts on a strong face, but he is really a very anxious guy. He has bad panic attacks, and we are really worried that he could do himself harm in jail."

Prior to being asked by the guys to visit Jerry, I had never visited anyone in jail, but I said that I would go the next day to visit Jerry. I never expected that offering to visit Jerry would evolve into a full-time jail chaplaincy and result in regular visits to the jail several days per week.

I called the jail the next morning to ask what the procedure was for visiting an inmate. I was told that visiting hours were 10 AM to noon and 1 to 3 PM, but that I had to be on the inmate's list of visitors in order to visit.

Who knew you had to have an "invitation" to visit someone in jail?

But that was the rule, and somehow I had to get word to Jerry to put me on his visitor's list. I was about to see firsthand how effectively and quickly the jailhouse grapevine worked. I drove over to Jerry's camp and told his friends that Jerry had to put me on his visitor list. Somehow that message was relayed from Jerry's friends outside the jail to Jerry inside the jail, and the answer came back from Jerry that he had put me on his list.

How in heaven's name did that happen and happen so quickly? I'm not sure I want to know.

Later that day, I arrived at the jail.

I was greeted by a lobby full of people waiting to visit inmates. There was obviously no dress code for visitors to the jail, and the clothing and appearances of the crowd were, at best, diverse.

Are that man's pants really going to stay up? Is that blouse cut that low to give the inmate a 'show'? Does that baby crawling on the dirty floor really have no clothing other than his diaper?

The mix of English, Spanish, and street slang was both loud and confusing.

I approached the glass window, showed my ID, and asked if I could visit Jerry. It seemed like the officer would take the rest of the day scanning up and down a list until she finally found my name on Jerry's list of visitors.

"The visitor stations are all full. It should be about half an hour.

Just take a seat, and we will call you."

I waited patiently on one of the hard plastic chairs. A kaleidoscope of sights and sounds swirled around me. Children were crying, visitors were losing their tempers as their impatience grew, and conversations were carried on in loud voices and in unlimited variations of street slang, Ebonics, and assorted profanities. Prodigious amounts of potato chips and a variety of junk foods were being consumed, and soft drinks were being guzzled out of quart bottles and oversized cups.

The odor of unchanged diapers and poor hygiene filled the air.

Cell phones rang incessantly, followed by loud conversations.

Folks, you don't need to shout into the phone. It works, and you can speak at normal levels!

Finally, the officer told me, "Go to Booth 28, pick up the phone, and wait until your prisoner comes on the screen."

If the noise and activity in the waiting room was intense, the noise and activity in the small phone room was "intense on steroids."

The room was filled with about thirty stations, which were nothing more than a three to four-foot section of a counter with a phone handset hanging on the wall next to a small TV screen. The screen was so yellowed and scratched that I wondered if it even worked. People were speaking loudly, and there were constant calls for officers as the screens went blank or folks couldn't hear on their headsets.

I picked up the phone as instructed and stared at the yellowed screen. Suddenly the screen lit up and was filled with bright

37

orange. It was obvious that the camera was focused on Jerry's chest and his bright orange jumpsuit, not on his face.

"Jerry, is that you?"

"Yes, Bob. I hear you but can't see you." Obviously, the camera on my end didn't work at all.

But, without seeing each other, we managed to communicate until my time was up, and I had to leave.

"Sorry buddy, all I saw was orange. Maybe next time we will be able to actually see each other," I said as I hung up the phone.

I walked back to the lobby, reflecting upon how truly meaningless the conversation with Jerry had been. Jerry and I couldn't see each other and had made no eye contact. We could barely hear the other over the noise in the room, and we certainly could not have had any personal or meaningful conversation.

What can I do to make this any better?

Chapter 10
THE CHAIN OF COMMAND

After my visit with Jerry, I walked back to the glass window where I had checked in. A Sheriff's officer in uniform and a man dressed in civilian clothes were behind the glass.

"Is there any way I can meet face-to-face with a prisoner?" I asked.

"Are you a doctor, lawyer, or minister?" the uniformed officer replied.

"No, I am not. I am a retired lawyer, but I no longer practice, and I am not here representing a client; those days are over. I am just a friend trying to visit a friend."

"Who are you visiting and why?" the officer asked.

I went through an explanation of Can We Help and told her how it came about that I wanted to visit with Jerry.

"The friends of the homeless are not likely to come to a jail to visit their friends—they tend to avoid law enforcement! And when a homeless person is taken into custody, their meager belongings are left at their camps and will disappear before they are released. I think I can help them adjust to incarceration and can also help them secure and protect their possessions," I explained.

"That's very nice of you, but I don't see how you can see them one on one. You'll have to use the phones like everyone else," the Sheriff's officer replied.

As I listened to what I was saying, I wondered what I was getting myself into. I had come to the jail to see one person, so why am I standing here trying to make arrangements to see others?

"I'm afraid I can't help you, but have a seat, and I will pass your request on to someone who may be available to talk to you."

Several minutes later, the steel door from the lobby into the jail opened, and the man who had been behind the window in street clothes emerged.

"Hi, I am Terry, the Head of Programming here in the jail. Tell me again who you are and what it is that you want to do."

Terry listened attentively while I again explained what Can We Help was doing with the homeless and why I had come over to visit Jerry. I went on to tell Terry about my visit with Jerry and how virtually meaningless it had been given the lack of any face-to-face contact and the very limited ability to actually communicate.

"If these folks really do have trouble adjusting to or accepting incarceration, maybe just a reassuring visit can be of some help."

"Do you intend to limit your visits to only the homeless?" Terry asked.

"Probably," I responded. "But, I honestly haven't thought that far ahead yet."

"I just feel that some of the homeless folks who end up here have big-time emotional and mental illnesses, and I think they could use a visit," I answered.

I repeated my concern that "others may not have had time to secure their camps and their belongings before being arrested, and I would like to help them safeguard their things while they are incarcerated."

40

We ended our conversation with polite handshakes, and although Terry was extremely attentive, I left feeling that I wouldn't hear anything further from him.

A few days later, I was pleasantly surprised when my phone rang, and it was Terry.

"Could you meet with me and the Sheriff's Department Chaplain for lunch?"

"Sure, when?"

"How about tomorrow at noon? Bono's on Route 1?" Terry responded.

The next day at noon, I slid into a booth where Terry and a man he introduced as the Sheriff's Department's professional Chaplain, Bryan, were already seated.

After exchanging pleasantries, Bryan began by saying, "Terry has told me a little bit about you, so why don't you tell me why you want to visit inmates."

I repeated the reasons which now flowed from me as if I had scripted them. I was able to answer every question that Bryan posed, but partway through the conversation, I thought to myself, *Lord, what are you doing? Why am I here? What am I getting myself into?*

At the end of our lunch, Bryan said that he wanted to set up a meeting with the Sheriff and me to see if the Sheriff would approve my request. With that, Bryan took a call, excused himself, and Terry and I continued the conversation.

Terry explained that although the jail had a wide variety of programs for the inmates, there was nothing directed specifically

41

to the homeless. Both he and Bryan had been looking for something that would be an appropriate outreach to homeless inmates.

Okay, Lord, this is getting serious. They may actually need me.

Several days later, Terry called to tell me that he, Bryan, and the Sheriff would meet with me the next day at the Sheriff's office.

I was warmly greeted by the Sheriff's receptionist and was ushered into the Sheriff's wood-paneled office furnished with beautiful leather furniture. I looked around and saw a typical variety of pictures of the Sheriff in full uniform with a number of dignitaries and various awards. But, what caught my attention was the Bible on the Sheriff's desk and the plaque on one wall honoring the Sheriff as the "Law Enforcement Officer of the Year." It had been given to him by an organization of Christian law enforcement officers.

Within a few minutes, the Sheriff came in and, just as Bryan had done, he told me that Terry had briefed him but that he wanted to hear firsthand about Can We Help and what I intended to be doing in his jail.

I am guessing that a good Sheriff with a competent staff had already vetted Can We Help, and probably me.

But, nonetheless, I went through it all again. What Can We Help was doing with the homeless, how many people it was serving, and how I had come to visit Jerry.

Have these guys scripted these questions? And are they cross-checking what I am telling them? Be careful and be accurate. These guys are professionals.

42

"Why do you think you can minister one on one to the inmates? You have no training as a Chaplain and no experience as a counselor," the Sheriff understandably asked.

"I don't really know if I can. You are correct that I have no training as a Chaplain or Counselor, but I do have a passion for these folks. I really feel that I have been led here, and I don't think that having this conversation is my doing or an accident," was all I could say.

After several more questions, the Sheriff stood up, extended his hand, and said, "Well, Mr. No Training, you better start to 'bone up' because you are about to become a Chaplain in my jail."

I didn't really catch the earlier reference to "his" jail, but the "my" jail this time around did not get past me.

The emphasis on the *'my'* told me that this man took his job and his jail seriously and would keep a close eye on what I would be doing in "his" jail.

The Sheriff instructed me to stop downstairs to be fingerprinted, fill out the forms for a background check, and, assuming that everything came back clear, arrange with Terry how to get started.

That evening I wrestled with myself about whether this was what I should be doing, and after a restless night, I resolved that I simply had to accept that all this was beyond my doing.

I had gone from simply taking a pot of spaghetti to a group of homeless men and women to running a non-profit to now being a Chaplain?

It was daunting and beyond me; I could not yet see a clear path forward, but I decided to give it a try.

Chapter 11
LEARN THE RULES

The interviews and approvals were complete, the fingerprinting and a mountain of forms had been completed, and I was simply waiting for the background check to be completed before I could begin my jail visits.

The phone rang. It was Terry.

"Everything came back clear. When can you start? How about tomorrow for orientation?"

I agreed to meet Terry at the jail the next morning.

Terry met me in the lobby and ushered me into his office to take my photo for an ID badge. Then he asked me to sit down.

 I was about to learn that jails are all about rules. Terry explained that the rules are there to safeguard visitors, to protect dangerous people from dangerous people, and to make certain that everything that occurs within those walls occurs pursuant to strict procedures. There can be no guesswork, no judgment calls. Everything Is done strictly by the rules.

"Okay, let's start at the beginning," Terry said.

"You must check in at the window, and you must show your ID each time you come. No ID, no entry.

Then place everything you have in your pockets or are carrying on the table. The officer will inspect each item, and if it can't go inside, they will hold it for you until you come back out.

After they inspect your belongings, they will ask you to raise your hands, and they will wand you for any metals."

"By the way, you are going to have to replace that Bible with a soft cover one; hardcovers can be used as a weapon and aren't allowed inside."

"Now, I'm going to give you a quick rundown of the 'Ten Commandments.' Every one of them is important. Please don't deviate from them," Terry instructed.

Rule #1: <u>Don't ever open any door on your own.</u>

"Don't ever open or try to open any door on your own. The officers will open the doors for you. You just push the buzzer… they will ask who you are and where you are going. Identify yourself and tell them precisely where you are going. Each set of officers will then pass you on to the next set of officers, that group will pass you along to the next group, and so forth until you get to where you are going."

Rule #2: <u>Stay on schedule.</u>

"We not only need to know where you are going but how long you intend to be there. If you spend more time than normal with someone or if you have to change where you are going for any reason, let someone know. We need to know exactly where you are at all times in case we have to extract you."

"Extract me?! What does that mean," I asked.

"You don't want to know… just be where you are supposed to be, and we'll handle the rest if and whenever necessary."

Rule #3: <u>Get to and stay at your destination, and when you leave, do so by the same route you used coming in.</u>

"Once you get inside, you can't be roaming around, and when you leave, go back out the exact same way you came in so we can

46

see and follow you. We can't have people roaming around in there or getting somewhere they can't be seen."

Rule #4: <u>No weapons and leave nothing behind.</u>

"Never carry anything that could be used as a weapon. No pen knives, no nail clippers, no pens or pencils that you give to the inmates. If you have a pen or pencil, keep it in your hand or pocket, don't even lay it on the table. An inmate can get the drop on you or an officer with something as simple as a pen or pencil."

"Do not bring anything in from anyone on the outside. There can be drugs impregnated on an innocent-looking piece of paper. What seems like a blank paper may also have things written on it with invisible ink."

If you do have something you want to leave with an inmate, give it to the officer first. They will inspect it and let you know if it can be given to the inmate."

Rule # 5: <u>Limit your jewelry, dress down, and don't give the inmates any personal information.</u>

"You don't want to give these folks the idea that you have any money or jewelry. They may not forget that when they get out.

Don't give them your home address."

Rule #6: <u>Never carry or relay a message from anyone on the outside or from inmate to inmate.</u>

"These folks are very good at communicating in ways that sound innocent but may not be. Sometimes, inmates are separated for a good reason... and we want to keep them separated and unable to communicate with each other."

"And, absolutely no messages from the outside to an inmate. You have no idea what they may be actually saying in what seems to be an innocent message."

Rule # 8: <u>Listen to and obey the officers.</u>

"There's zero tolerance for not obeying an officer's directive."

"You must absolutely and totally comply with what the officers tell you or ask of you. They may be dealing with a serious situation, and they need your complete cooperation."

"Whatever they tell you, or no matter how long you have to wait to see the inmate, just go with it or move on."

Rule #9: <u>Don't touch the inmates.</u>

"No hugs, no arms around their shoulders, nothing that would allow you or them to pass anything. Everything must be in full view of the cameras and the officers monitoring the cameras."

Rule # 10: <u>Respect.</u>

"Treat each inmate with respect. Most of these folks have been disrespected, abused, or mistreated for most of their lives. A little respect and showing them a little dignity will go a long way. On the other hand, disrespecting them can create a nasty situation."

"Okay, any questions? And, remember that someone's life or safety may depend on whether or not you are following the rules."

Terry took me through the first set of doors from the lobby into the jail. He showed me the elevator and how to operate it, and he took me up to the second floor.

"Access to all the cell blocks is from the second floor—each of those hallways goes to a different wing, and the wings are all numbered with big black numbers on the walls."

"This desk is for people coming in to work with or visit the inmates. There are bibles on the shelf, there are these small cups of wine and a wafer for communion, and any daily instructions or notices will be posted on this bulletin board."

"Here is a list of homeless guys who came in over the last week. Why don't you pick someone and get started on your first visit? Pick anyone you want and get started."

Get started, oh my, get started! You mean in the real jail with real inmates?

I reviewed the list and was relieved to see a name that I recognized.

John was an older man who lived on a bench in downtown Seaside Beach Park. He was a panhandler and a confirmed pothead who was very proud of the fact that he used nothing but marijuana. But he used plenty of it.

I'll get started with John, he knows me, and that will be an easy start.

I went down the hallway to cell block number 3 and pushed the buzzer as Terry had instructed.

"Who is it, and what's your business?"

"I am Chaplain Bob to see John."

Buzz, click, the door opened a crack, and the voice on the speaker said, "Come on down, have a seat, and we will bring him up."

While I was waiting, an officer came up and asked if I was

49

new.

"Brand new, first day, first visit," I responded.

"Good to have you, and don't forget..." and the officer briefly repeated the rules.

John soon appeared, and he looked better than I was used to seeing him on the street or at our meals. He was clean-shaven, his hair was cut and combed, he had showered, and although he wore an orange jumpsuit, it was clean.

On the outside, John washed himself in the park's public restroom, he had no way to wash his clothes, and a haircut was a luxury that he could not afford, or if he did have money for a haircut, he preferred to use it for his marijuana.

John was surprised to see me.

"What did you do to get yourself in here?" I asked.

A no, no, I would later learn. Don't ask inmates why they were there or for any details of their crimes. The intake sheet will tell me their charges, and that was all I needed to know.

Since I was not really a clergyman hearing confessions and was not a lawyer, anything an inmate told me would not be privileged and could be used against them or could subject me to being subpoenaed as a witness against the innate or others.

John began, "It's cold out there, and I wasn't feeling all that great. All I have to do is walk down downtown and take a leak in front of some tourists. That's a surefire way to get picked up for public indecency or some other horse shit charge that will get me a warm bed, some good food, and a chance to clean up and rest up."

John was what I would come to know as "a professional inmate."

Like many of the homeless, he knew that every several months he could get himself arrested for a minor offense and spend several weeks in jail. He would get medical care, rest, be able to stay warm if it was winter, and get three square meals a day to get him back on his feet. Coming in and out of jail for John and some others was a very normal and regular, if not essential, part of their lives.

Since they had given me the title *Chaplain,* I thought that I had better get about being *Chaplain-like.*

"Can we read some scripture together, or would you like me to pray with me?"

"Sure," John quickly replied. "That's the one thing I miss in here. The church services are lousy. When I'm out, I like to go to the Salvation Army services and get a nice hot breakfast after the service. These folks don't even bring you a cookie."

I didn't think it was necessary to explain to John that we were not allowed to bring anything into the jail, so I just let his comment about the cookie slide.

When we finished, John told me that he had left his bicycle chained in the bike rack at the AA hall and asked if I could pick it up and safeguard it for him until he got out. Being mindful of the rules, I told John that I would check and see if that would be allowed.

On my way out, I relayed John's request to Terry. Terry just chuckled a bit, telling me that "I would learn," and then said, "Yes," that would be fine.

"My guess is that by the time John gets out, he will have forgotten all about the bike you are holding for him and will find a way to get someone else to give him a new bike, but have at it if you wish."

Yep, sounds like John does know the ropes and has been through this before, but I want to show him that I am here to try to help him, so I will go pick up his bike on my way home.

Just as Terry had predicted, the bike sat in the Can We Help offices for several months despite several efforts to have John come to pick it up after he had been released. When I finally saw John at one of our meals with a shiny new bike, we gave his old bike to another homeless man. Lesson learned.

Chapter 12
NANCY

When I first began the jail ministry I was not permitted to visit women. Then one day, a male inmate asked me to check on his girlfriend who had been picked up with him and may be in withdrawal.

I relayed the request to see her to the Sheriff and it was initially denied.

"Wait a minute. I will be in a 12 x 12 room with cameras in the ceiling and open speakers that can be used to hear everything we are discussing. Just what could happen between a man and woman in those circumstances?" I replied back.

"Point well taken. Let's give it a try," was the Sheriff's response.

I visited with the lady, and she was in withdrawal. She welcomed the visit, and the word spread quickly among the female inmates. I soon had an increasing number of women requesting a visit.

When will I learn? Stop asking for more work.

After that, the lists of men and women had grown beyond what I could manage. I had to reduce my visits to ten minutes each in order to see everyone, and ten minutes was not enough time to have a meaningful visit.

All of these jail visits started because I could not have a meaningful visit with Jerry, and now I am right back to not being able to have meaningful visits with the people.

At about that time, a friend started organizing fundraising breakfasts for Can We Help. At one of the breakfasts, Can We Help invited other community organizations to nominate one of their volunteers for recognition.

The Salvation Army nominated Nancy and her husband, who had worked tirelessly taking breakfasts and lunches to the homeless with the Army's food truck.

After the breakfast was completed, the award winners stayed for a photo session. I was making small talk with Nancy and her husband, and to my complete surprise, Nancy told me that her husband was going to continue with the food truck but that she was looking for a new challenge.

"What are you thinking about as a new challenge?" I asked.

I was stunned when she told me that she had been praying for an opportunity to do a jail ministry and asked me if I knew anyone who was doing a jail ministry and may need help.

Lord, what are you doing this time?

In my mind, I heard His immediate response: "You said you needed help. I have just sent you help. Talk with the lady."

"Can we have breakfast or lunch to talk about this?" I asked.

"Sure," Nancy responded. "How about breakfast tomorrow at Bono's?"

Bono's! Where the jail ministry began with Terry and Bryan. Cut it out, Lord. This is too much!!

Without hesitation, I agreed to meet Nancy the next morning and made it a priority to get to Bono's early to get the same booth that Terry, Bryan, and I had shared.

When Nancy arrived, we ordered coffee and our breakfasts, exchanged some pleasantries, and I began to explain to her what I was doing in the jail.

She was flabbergasted and had no idea that I had been doing a jail ministry. She listened attentively but responded that she felt completely unqualified to do one on one visits. She just wanted to join up with a group that went into the jail to do church services or Bible studies.

"I could never sit one on one with people. I'm afraid that I wouldn't know what to say," Nancy explained.

"I can connect you with some people who do Sunday and mid-week church services in the jail, but why not try the one on one meetings? If you don't feel comfortable, you can always join up with the group that does the services," I suggested.

I then shared with Nancy my own misgivings and feelings of inadequacy, which had resulted in my "argument with God" and Ashlee's words of wisdom telling me why I was there and how much the ladies appreciated not just being told what they should or should not be doing.

"I can tell you two things, Nancy. First, these folks aren't looking for a scholarly, theological discussion, and second, I can assure you that if you just keep an open mind, listen to what they are asking, and rely on the Lord to lead you, it will all work out."

Without hesitation, Nancy replied, "If you are willing to help me and are patient, let's give it a go."

Nancy went through the vetting, approval, and background

check processes and, within a few weeks, met me at the jail, ready to start work.

To say that Nancy was a natural would be understating her abilities. She had a deeply compassionate nature, was an extraordinarily quick learner, and her faith was rock solid. She had a total commitment to the gospel message and an insatiable desire to share it with anyone who would listen.

"But, how do I put all this together? I don't know anything about addiction, so how can I give them the advice that they may need," she asked.

"Here's what I have learned. It is not us. It is not our knowledge or our expertise that will help these folks. In fact, these people have had enough of people telling them what to do and how to do it."

"Their lives have fallen so hard and so far that they need to be reborn, regenerated in the most basic sense of those words. We can't do that for them. AA can't do it for them. Parents or family members can't do it for them. All of those things can be crutches and can help, but we need to show them how to turn their lives over to the Lord and let Him do it for them."

"That sounds heavy. How do we get them to do that?" she asked.

"Nancy, I have no training, and I have no experience. All I know is that God has taken me down a completely unbelievable path to get here. Trust Him, not yourself,"

In our first few times together, Nancy expressed amazement that, in her opinion, I always seemed to know exactly what to say to people.

"Nancy, honestly, as I have told you, it is not me. I never know what we are going to encounter or how I am going to respond. As we walk down the hallway, my prayer is that the Lord will give me the words I will need. I suggest that you leave your prepared lessons (which she had obviously spent considerable time organizing and preparing) at home and just see where He takes you. He knows far better than us what these folks need, and He will not let us mislead them if we simply trust in Him. If He has put it in your heart to come in here to help these people, He will give you the tools you need. Just keep asking Him to give you those tools. He won't fail us if we stay true to Him."

The relief on Nancy's face was palpable. "Here I have been thinking that you are always so well prepared and that I also need to have something prepared."

"Not so. I keep telling you that this is not about us or what we think these folks need. It is about allowing ourselves to be His messengers."

Nancy soon became a stalwart to the men and women we visited. She and I began dividing the list of men and women and began seeing them separately so that we could see twice as many. For the *tough ones,* the ones who needed more time, we would both schedule to see them even if we had to come back in the evenings.

Chapter 13
AN ANGEL'S POEM

"What is this, and where did it come from?" I exclaimed as I opened and read what I found lying on my desk in a plain white envelope.

"Who wrote this, and where did it come from?"

It cannot be from the jail. It doesn't have the notation on the envelope advising that it is sent from an inmate. Where did it come from, and who wrote it?

No one in the office had any idea where it had come from and said it must have been slid under the door since it had no stamp, no address on the envelope, and no return address. The staff had just assumed it was a donation or letter asking for some kind of assistance.

"Who is Delaney Farrell? That name doesn't even ring a bell to me," I asked as I read the document with trembling hands.

As I read what Delaney had written, it sounded eerily similar to the stories that I had been hearing from the ladies in the jail. Delaney had written:

Funny, I don't remember any good dope days. I remember *walking for miles in a dope fiend haze.*

I remember sleeping in houses that had no electricity. I remember being called a junkie but couldn't accept it.

*I remember hanging out in abandos (*tenements, trailers, or any structure that was abandoned by its former occupants*) that were empty and dark. I remember shooting up in the bathroom and* *falling out in the park.*

I remember nodding out in front of my sister's kids. I remember not remembering half the things I did.

I remember the dope man's time frame—ten more minutes. I remember those days being so sick that I just wanted to end it.

I remember birthdays and holiday celebrations and all the things I missed during my incarceration.

I remember my sister's cry and my dad having to break down the door. I remember the look on his face when I opened my eyes, thinking that today was the day that his baby had died.

I remember blaming myself when my mom decided to leave. I remember the guilt I felt in my chest, making it hard to breathe.

I remember caring so much, not knowing how to show it, and I know to this day that she probably don't even know it.

I remember feeling like I lost all hope. I remember giving up my body for the next bag of dope.

I remember only causing pain, destruction, and harm. I remember the track marks the needles left on my arm.

I remember the slow break up of my home. I remember thinking my family would be better off if I just left them alone.

I remember looking in the mirror at my sickly complexion. I remember not recognizing myself in my own damn reflection.

I remember obsessing over my next score. But what I remember the most is getting down on my knees and asking God to save me cuz I don't want to do this no more.

Who is this person, and how did her beautiful poem get to me? I asked out loud.

This is the most beautiful poem I have ever read.

I quickly Googled Delaney Farrell. I learned that she was a young lady, just 23 years old, from mid-state Pennsylvania, who had been struggling with addiction for several years. After several failed attempts to rehab, she appeared to be sober and doing well, or so everyone thought. She was even working as a housekeeper in a motel near her hometown.

Then on July 1, 2017, suddenly and without warning, she was found dead from an overdose in a room at the motel.

It turned out that Delaney had relapsed and that she and over fifty other people had been sold heroin laced with carfentanil, a drug used to tranquilize large animals.

Tragically, for Delaney, her dose had been fatal.

Delaney had written this beautiful poem describing her thoughts, feelings, and experiences as an addict, and when her mother found it after her death, she courageously published it in Delaney's obituary.

It perfectly described and summarized everything that I had been hearing from the young addicts I had been seeing in the jail.

But how did it find its way to South Florida?

I continued to research Delaney and found that she had been a bright, happy, talented 18-year-old from central Pennsylvania who her friends considered to be the life of the party. She was full of laughter, always smiling, and a very, very engaging young lady.

Sounds just like many of the ladies I was visiting.

But, at age 18, her world changed when she was introduced to opioids by a friend at a party.

Or by an unscrupulous doctor or "pain clinic," as had happened to some of the young women I knew.

Her life quickly spiraled out of control, and she fell hard and fast into the bottomless pit of addiction.

I have heard that story a number of times in the jail.

Through this poem, Delaney told me exactly what she and all these other struggling young women were feeling and experiencing.

Delaney could have been just another tragic statistic in the world of the opioid epidemic. But somehow, her poem had found its way to me in Seaside Beach, Florida, and was about to become an important part of our ministry.

"Listen to this and think about it," I said to the volunteers in the office.

"This is a real person speaking from her heart directly to all of us. This is a real person whose life was controlled for almost five years by heroin and then violently ripped away from her by heroin, and she tells us that she "can't remember any good dope days..." not one good day!

"Isn't that absolutely profound!"

For the first time, I felt that I could finally empathize with and understand an addict's feelings, how their lives were destroyed and controlled by heroin, and the anguish they experience on a daily basis.

I would no longer have to be concerned that I had no knowledge of addiction, that I didn't know how an addict felt about their addiction, or that I could not identify with what the young ladies were feeling.

Delaney just explained it all in the best of terms, and God had somehow seen to it that her message traveled from Pennsylvania to South Florida and onto my desk.

Lord, you are indeed in control here. You have put me in this place. You sent me Ashlee when I needed her, you sent me Nancy, and now you have sent me Delaney.

All I could think of was the great hymn, "Trust and Obey," for there is no other way... just trust and obey.

Chapter 14
DID YOU WRITE THIS?

It was a beautiful day. The sun was shining brightly, the sky was a cloudless blue, and the summer humidity had not yet arrived in South Florida.

The beautiful skies and weather matched the joy in my heart as I made several copies of Delaney's poem and prepared to take them on my visit to the jail.

As I checked in, I gave the copies to the officer and asked her, "Please check these out to see if it is okay for me to leave them with some of the ladies I am going to see today. I printed them myself and can attest that the paper is clean."

The officer disappeared with the papers and came back with copies she had made on their own copy paper.

"You're good to go now, Chaplain. I recopied them on our paper, so I know it is clean. I will let the officers upstairs know that you are allowed to leave copies with your ladies. May I ask who wrote this? It is really powerful."

"An angel," I replied.

Tracey was the first lady that I was scheduled to see that day.

Tracey was a very shy and not very articulate young woman. Conversations with Tracey were difficult, and her answers were almost always one-word—"Yea," "No," or "Maybe."

I began...

"Tracey, I found this on my desk the other day, and I am not sure where it came from. Is this something you may have given me the last time we visited?"

A blank look and a "Huh?" was Tracey's response.

"Just take a minute to read it over, and tell me if it is something you wrote."

I sat back and gave Tracey time to read Delaney's poem. As she read, her face changed from a deadpan look of complete disinterest to one of utter amazement.

"Who wrote this, and where the hell did you get it?" she asked.

I explained what it was, described how I had gotten it, and shared with her what I had been able to learn about Delaney.

"This bitch nailed it," Tracey exclaimed. "That's me. That's all of us. We've all walked that same rough road."

"I don't think I can remember any good dope days, either, and my family is certainly a wreck because of me. I've been tricking for a couple of years and have nothing to show for it except a bunch of needle tracks on my arms and legs."

"And this last line… 'I don't want to do this no more'…. that's me. Except I usually go one step further… I usually ask God to just let me die."

"So, Tracey, I know it is hard for you to talk about yourself and your life. Would it help if, in future visits, we use Delaney's poem and pretend you wrote it," I suggested.

"That way, we can go through your own experiences without you struggling with how to put your thoughts into words. Delaney has done that for you."

"Works for me," was Tracey's enthusiastic reaction.

And I believe it will work for many others, I thought.

Chapter 15
THE MISSING LINK and A NEW MESSAGE

After my "argument with God," Ashlee's advice not to tell them what to do or not do, and now Delaney's poem, Nancy and I were developing our own approach to working with the ladies. It was a steep learning curve, but we were climbing it slowly and steadily.

However, there was still something missing.

We watched as too many relapsed.

We watched as too many recycled over and over again into the jail.

We saw that the 12-Step programs were invaluable, but even the diligent attendees were relapsing at too high of a rate.

We understood that expensive inpatient programs were beyond the financial reach of most of our ladies.
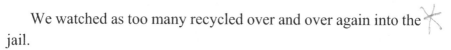

Ashlee had taught us that they did not need more people telling them what to do. They had been doing the same things for years without success.

So what could we offer the ladies that would bring them a new perspective and, perhaps, a higher degree of success in finding long-term sobriety?

Nancy rhetorically asked me, "What are we missing?"

"I don't know, Nancy. All I know is that God has put us in this position, and we have to trust that He will show us the way," I replied.

"I don't see the answer yet, but I know that we just have to get ourselves out of the way and trust Him."

Easy to say, not so easy to do, I thought as I said goodnight to Nancy and walked to my car.

That evening, I was reading the Bible. I knew that I had to meet with Ashlee the next morning, so I decided to reread Romans 7, which we had discussed in our last session.

Paul's words suddenly took on new meaning. I read and reread what Paul had written:

*that he did not understand what he was doing

*that he could not do what he knew he should be doing

*that he hated doing the things he was doing but couldn't stop doing them

Isn't that what every addict has been telling us?

They all knew that they shouldn't be doing drugs, but they did.

They all know they don't want to do drugs, yet they continue to do them.

As I read further, I thought about Paul telling us that he had "a thorn in his flesh."

What was that "thorn"? Could it have been an addiction?

We'll never know, and Paul doesn't tell us what the 'thorn' was, but don't all of our ladies also have a 'thorn'? The thorn of addiction.

Paul concludes by calling himself "a wretched man."

Ouch, wretched. That is a strong term, but wasn't that what Delaney was telling us about how she felt?

I read further to try to see if Paul told us how he combatted his "thorn."

Paul pleaded with God to remove the thorn from his side, but God refused, saying that by allowing the thorn to remain in Paul, he would see his weaknesses and would rely on the strength of God to overcome those weaknesses.

We had been praying with the ladies that God would remove their addictions—their thorns—from them. Maybe that was the wrong prayer. Maybe we should just be helping them to accept their "thorn" of addiction and to rely on the strength of God to manage it.

I couldn't wait to share this new insight with Nancy, and we met early the next morning to discuss this new approach.

"That's it," Nancy exclaimed.

"We, and they, may just need to accept the fact that, for whatever reason, God has given them the 'thorn of addiction,' and maybe they just need to accept it and rely on the strength of God to control it for them."

"Let's get to the jail and try this out with some of the ladies," I suggested.

The first lady they visited was June.

June had been a hardcore addict for over ten years, but as many said, she was now committed to getting clean.

Her fear was that since she had failed so many times before, she was destined to fail again. Like many of the others, her life had been filled with good intentions but only short periods of sobriety followed by a relapse back into active drug use.

She just couldn't stop, no matter how much she hated it and how hard she tried.

What a perfect segue into their newly developed message.

We asked June to open her Bible and read Romans 7. She began reading but couldn't finish it.

"That's me! That's what it is like! I want to stop so badly. I know it's wrong, but no matter how I try, I just can't stop," June said through her tears.

"Okay, June, let's try to see how Paul overcame his 'thorn.' How did he overcome it?"

"It's right here. He tells us that it was only with the help of God," June replied.

"But I don't even know what that means, much less how to do it. How do I get this help from God, and why would Jesus be worried about me and the mess that I have created?"

"Well, let's go back to more of Paul's writings and see how he got the help he needed.

"Here, in Ephesians, he tells us about putting on the 'armor of God' for protection against Satan's temptations. I want you to read these verses and see if they may help you. Maybe, when you feel tempted to use, you just put on that armor of God—the breastplate of righteousness, the shield of faith, the sword... the word of God—and fight Satan with the confidence that you are now protected by the armor of God."

69

June wasn't buying it at first, but she did want to hear more.

June wasn't ready to accept the Bible as being anything more than a nice story, and she certainly wasn't ready to rely on it to control her addiction.

What is it about all of us that makes us reject the simplest of notions and think that we somehow have to figure it out on our own? Don't we all think that unless we can understand it, it must not be true? June was no different than most of us.

But it was a start. We had planted the seeds and now had to just wait and see what happened.

As we left June and walked down the hallway, Nancy and I both questioned ourselves. Did we really trust that this approach would work? Some ladies were just not going to accept it. Some were non-believers, some had fallen far, far away from their beliefs, and some were outright hostile to the Bible.

"Wait just a minute… Satan is whispering in our ears again," Nancy said.

"The real question is not whether they believe or accept it yet. The real question is, do we believe it, and do we believe that it is a solution for these ladies? If we do believe that, it is our task to just lay it out for them."

"Bingo, I think we have found the missing link, and now we have a new —even though it is a very old—message to share with the ladies," I responded.

Damn, I am a slow learner. Forgive me, Lord.

Chapter 16
OPIOIDS COME TO DINNER

It was a usual Thursday night, and I was helping to serve the meal to the homeless on the Seaside Beach Causeway when my phone buzzed. It was a text from Sandra: "Get over here to the meal on Indian Street ASAP. We have a problem with Mandy."

Mandy was a homeless woman who lived in a camp with several men. She had been a regular at the Thursday evening meals since they started. Generally, she was a very pleasant woman, but she could be a problem on any given night. For the past few months, she had been coming to the meals under the influence of something but steadfastly denied that it was drugs.

"What the hell are you all over me about? Sure, I had a couple of beers when I got home from work. You guys have your cocktails when you get home, don't you? So why can't I?" was her response to any questions concerning her condition.

In the past several weeks, she had begun losing weight. She often had dry heaves, which she attributed to some bad food she had eaten at lunch. Her personality was becoming very argumentative and even combative. Our biggest concern was that she had begun developing open sores on her arms. When anyone asked her about the sores, she said they were from the strong cleaning fluids that she used on her job. However, the sores looked, to the untrained eye, to be abscesses from the use of dirty needles.

When I arrived at Indian Street, I found that Mandy had locked herself in the restroom inside the Labor Hall. She was shouting at or arguing with some imaginary villain or creature inside the restroom and would not open the door, insisting that she would not come out until Tony arrived.

"Why do you need Tony?" I asked through the locked door.

"He's bringing me medicine for these damn heaves," Mandy replied. "I'm not coming out there and making a fool out of myself puking all over the place."

"What medicine do you need, Mandy? Maybe we can send someone over to Walgreens to pick it up for you," I tried to reason.

"Tony knows what I need, and he went to get it. He should be here by now."

Tony was one of the men Mandy lived with in the woods. He was suspected to be both a drug user and a small-time dealer. It was pretty obvious what "medicine" Tony was bringing to her. By this point, it seemed like Mandy was probably in the early stages of withdrawal and desperately needed Tony's "medicine."

Tom was a homeless man who was a regular at the Thursday meals. Can We Help had gotten Tom life-saving cancer treatment through Volunteers in Medicine, and now he was paying it forward. Tom had an old van, and he helped transport people to Social Security, the VA, or Volunteers in Medicine.

When I arrived at Indian Street, Tom asked me to meet him around the front of the building, out of the sight and earshot of the others.

"Mandy needs help," Tom said. "She's been in bad shape for several weeks, and Tony has been controlling her by controlling her dope. He gives her just enough to keep her high but not enough to prevent her from working or providing for him and the boys."

"What's she using?" I asked.

"Straight mainline heroin," Tom replied.

"What can we do?" I asked.

"Nothing if she won't let us, but if she will listen to anyone, it is probably you, Bob. So get her out of that damn bathroom before Tony gets here and see if she will come to my camp for the night. I can then drive her to Volunteers in Medicine first thing in the morning."

We went back around to the back of the building. By that time, Mandy's shouts and screams had driven almost everyone else away.

The other guests anticipated that the police would be on their way, and most of them didn't want to be anywhere around when the police arrived.

Our first task was to get Mandy out of the restroom without causing more drama. Tom suggested a solution.

"Tell her that Tony has shown up with 'medicine' but that he won't come up since someone may have called the police. Tell her to come on out, and we will take her back to him."

"We've got nothing to lose, so let's go," I responded.

"Mandy, Tony is here, but he won't come up here to the hall. He's afraid the cops are on their way. He has your package back at your camp. Come on out."

Just as Tom had predicted, Mandy quieted down and came out.

I put both of my arms on her shoulders and said, "Mandy, I'm sorry I lied to you, Tony is not here, but we had to get you out so we could talk, so come on, let's take a walk and talk."

"Mandy, you are in bad shape, and I am tired of hearing about the cleaning solution and watching you become a skeleton. You are in the death grip of Mr. Heroin, and if we don't get you help, you may not be long for this world. Let's get you up to Volunteers in Medicine and get those sores checked out in the morning."

Surprisingly Mandy acknowledged that she needed help and agreed to meet Tom in the morning.

"Better yet, why don't you go with Tom back to his camp and stay the night there," I suggested.

She wanted no part of that and insisted on staying at her own camp but promised that she could meet Tom in the morning.

The next morning Mandy was predictably a no-show, and she disappeared for the next several weeks. She didn't come to the meals, and no one seemed to know anything about her. Even Tony claimed that he hadn't seen her.

After several weeks, her name unexpectedly showed up on the list of new inmates in the jail.

Nancy and I went to visit Mandy, but she was barely able to walk into the conference room. She was in serious withdrawal. She was shaking, sweating, and seemed about to go into convulsions. The officers assured me that she was through the worst of it, but neither Nancy nor I could make any sense of what she was babbling.

Our only option was to send her back down to her cell to suffer through the rest of her withdrawal.

A few days later, I went to visit Mandy again. She was through her withdrawal, cleaned up, and after a few days of good food that she could keep down, she looked and sounded like a different person.

"You know I am going to be here a while. They've got me on an intent to distribute charge. That new guy that was hanging around the meals was a Narc, and he nailed me when I tried to sell him a bag. I've learned my lesson, and I don't want to go back to the woods. I don't want to go back to Tony. My son will take me to his home once I get out of here."

Mandy seldom told the truth and always had an angle, so I was skeptical that she had come to that epiphany or that her son had even spoken to her, much less agreed to take her into his home.

"Let's deal with that when it comes time for your release," I suggested. "In the meantime, why don't you just begin meeting with Nancy or me, and let's see how things go by the time you are released."

"I told some other girls down there that you came to see me when I first came in, and I knew that you would come back. Some of them would like to see you. Will you see them?"

"Sure, I will if they put in a request to see me."

"I told them you are a no-bullshit guy and will tell them like it is… and all that religion stuff that you talk about wouldn't be so bad for them either. I'm going to get them ladies up here to see you, and maybe you can help them get off these damn drugs just like you are trying to help me."

Mandy spent almost a year in the county jail, awaiting the disposition of her charges. During her incarceration, God used her as an ambassador to send other addicts to Nancy and me.

Those women would then refer even more women to us so that by the end of Mandy's time in jail, we had a full schedule of female addicts we were seeing.

Mandy was finally released and told me that she was, in fact, going to live with her son.

Nancy and I offered to have Can We Help buy her a bus ticket, but she assured us that transportation to her son's home in Sebastian, Florida, was something she could take care of on her own.

At the following week's meal, Tom asked me if he had heard anything from Mandy.

"Nothing," I replied. "I haven't seen her since she left the jail."

Several months passed before Mandy reappeared. She came to town for her final appointment with her probation officer and came to one of the Thursday meals to say hello and thank everyone for their help and support.

She looked like a new person–indeed, she was a new person!

She had been sober since she left jail, she was living with her son, she had a job, and she was proud to tell us that she was about to become a grandmother.

Not a person could believe that this was the same woman who had locked herself in the bathroom.

Mandy had not only used her time in jail to rebuild her own life but had brought many other women to us.

Another lesson learned. He will bring folks to us that he wants us to meet with and will do so in the most unexpected ways.

Chapter 17
DEVI and HER MOTHER

New ladies continued coming to us each week. We often did not know them and never knew what to expect.

Little did we know that today we would meet someone with a story unlike any we had ever heard before or since.

The first new person that came through the door this day was an unusually well-coiffed and well-groomed young woman.

"Hi, I am Devalia, but you can call me Devi."

She looked to be about 30 and made a very dramatic first impression. I wondered how she kept herself so neat and put-together in this place.

Her jet-black hair was pulled tightly back into a bun. Her eyes were a beautiful green but were filled with distrust and anger. Her posture and mannerisms were rigid, and her upright body stood almost at military attention.

"I'm Bob, and this is Nancy. We are awfully glad to meet you. What can we do for you?"

"I have heard the girls talking about you guys. They say that you know a lot about Jesus. I want to ask you some things about him. Is that okay?"

"Of course, Devi. What do you want to know about Jesus?"

"First of all, I just want to know who he is."

"I'm sorry. Do you mean that you don't believe in Jesus, that you would like to learn more about him, or that you literally don't know who he is?" Nancy asked.

"I really don't know who he is —was he some kind of an emperor or king? And why do the girls make such a big deal about him? I have sort of heard about him, but I don't know very much about him because my mother is a bitch," Devi told us.

"Devi, let's not start out bashing your mother or anyone else. Let's talk about you," I interjected.

"Don't you think that it is important that my mother is a witch?" Devi asked.

This time I heard the 'W' that I had mistaken for a 'B.'

"What do you mean when you say that your mother is a witch?"

"I mean that she is a witch. We live in a coven with other witches, men, and women. And, we all worship Satan just like you worship your Gods."

I was tempted to correct her and say… God, not Gods. But not just yet.

"When mom was about my age, she started heavily using LSD. That was a big deal back then. She and her friends then started communal living in an old mansion in Los Angeles. Somehow the whole commune turned into Satan worshippers, and they moved to an old ghost town in Nevada. That's where I grew up," Devi explained.

"We lived there until my grandparents tried to get me away from my mother and the commune. My mother took off with me to get away from them. We ended up in Florida and hooked up with a small coven commune near Daytona."

"How did you get here from California and manage to find another coven in Daytona?" I inquired.

"The internet. There are plenty of devil worship websites on the internet. The Church of Satan, the Temple of Set, and the Church of Satanic Liberation have churches and covens everywhere. You can always find one near you."

Mom found one she liked and thought it was far enough away from my grandparents to be safe. We hitchhiked across the country from truck stop to truck stop. It's not hard for two women to get a ride in exchange for some creature comforts.

"Mom is really into the devil worship thing. It's been her whole adult life. She even named me after the devil—Devalia. She doesn't believe in God and thinks that the devil controls or should control the world."

At this point, I took a deep breath.

Is this for real, or is this the product of a mentally ill young lady? Only one way to find out.

"How about I just listen, and you tell me what it's like to have been raised by a witch and to worship the devil."

"Then you listen while I tell you about my life as a Christian and worshiping Jesus."

"Does that sound fair to you?"

"Sure."

"First of all, you have to understand that I never knew any other life, so what we were doing wasn't strange or unusual to me," Devi began.

"I thought the devil was God, just like you think that your Jesus is God."

Devi continued...

"It wasn't a bad life. There really were quite a few kids my age who came and went. It was a free-spirited lifestyle. Most of the women slept with different men all the time. I had the 'honor' of losing my virginity to one of the priests when I was just 13. To be chosen to sleep with a priest was a high honor. I became one of his favorites. I stayed with him until I was about 18, when he decided he wanted a younger girl."

"Did you go to school?" I asked.

"Hell no, they didn't want us anywhere outside the commune, so we were all home-schooled... if you want to call it that. There was a lady in the commune who said she was a teacher in her prior life. When she wasn't tripping, she tried to teach us. She wasn't very good, so I don't read very well and can't do any numbers."

"What did the priests or your mother tell you about Jesus?"

"They told us that if we ever said that word, we would get whipped, and they meant it."

"Why do you want to learn about Jesus now?"

"Because the girls down there who say they know Jesus are different. They aren't like the rest of us. So, I want to know what is so special about this guy."

"Do you consider yourself to be an addict?" I asked.

"Of course. I can't recall a time when I wasn't using drugs. It started with marijuana, then a little LSD, then Meth, and now my drug of choice is heroin. I love it, and I'll do it anyway I can get it into me. I sniff it, I smoke it, but I really love needles. That is the fastest and the best high you can get.

"We girls in the commune were supposed to do whatever we could to help get money. I wasn't into hooking, so I figured out ways to con men. It is ridiculous what men will give you if they think they are going to get laid. The trick was getting their money and getting away before you had to perform."

"The guys would knock off drug stores because the sleazy stores dealt in cash and always had plenty of it on hand. They also had more pills than most big chain pharmacies. The boys would find drug stores in bad neighborhoods that were filling bogus prescriptions. They would stick them up at the end of the day when they had plenty of cash in their flimsy little safes. It was dangerous, and the drug store owners had guns, but if the guys could get past that, the stores weren't about to call the cops and trigger an investigation into their operations."

I needed time to let all this soak in.

"Devi, I sure am going to enjoy telling you who Jesus is and can't wait to hear more about your life. But right now, I have to see the next lady on my list. How about we start next week?"

"I've got time. I'll be in here for a year or so, and I think they may even file more charges against me. They want me to tell them what I know about the group up in Daytona, but I am not about to tell them anything. Let them figure it out for themselves," Devi answered.

"They've got me on assault and battery with intent to kill my boyfriend, who deserved to die for what he did to me. But there is

81

no way he is going to show up and testify... the coven will take care of that. They will never let him testify. As soon as the state's attorney figures that out, they will offer me a plea deal to a lower charge, and I'll get out for time served."

The next week we began with Devi starting with the book of Genesis and reading about how God created the heavens and the earth.

Devi was far from a willing learner.

She argued with me about just about everything we read. She told me all that stuff was "nonsense," no one could make the world in seven days, and she questioned how I could believe any of it.

But, as time went on, she began to soften and became more inquisitive.

She gradually wanted to learn more. She said that she had begun to pray and do devotions with the other women.

Although she lacked a formal education, she was very bright with a highly inquisitive mind and asked great questions. Because of her limited reading abilities, I found bible storybooks that were within her ability to read.

After several months, Devi's entire demeanor and even her appearance changed. The distrust and anger were gone from her eyes. Her body language changed, and she seemed relaxed, not so stiff and severe.

Devi hadn't had any visits from her mother but said that she had been writing to her. She had actually been telling her mother what she had been learning about Jesus.

Her mother was apparently upset about all "this nonsense that these people are putting in your head" and had scheduled a time to come visit Devi "to get all that foolishness out of my head."

Devi was very anxious about her mother's first visit and asked me what she should tell her.

"When in doubt, tell the truth. Tell her what you have been doing, what you have learned, and what effect it has had on you. Just tell her how you are feeling and how you think you have changed."

Expecting that her mother was going to reprimand her, she was pleasantly surprised that her mother actually complimented her. She told Devi that she seemed like a different person. She said it was nice to see that she didn't have that dark look in her eyes and to see her smile.

Shortly after her first visit with her mother, Devi asked me what she had to do to take that "communion thing" that the girls talked about.

"Just ask, I always carry a few small communion cups that the jail provides, and we can take communion right now if you wish."

"Don't we need a priest or a preacher to do that?" Devi asked.

"Some would say that we do, but I don't agree with that."

"Although we most certainly should never take communion disrespectfully and must always do it reverently and in sincere memory of Jesus, I don't think it has to be given to us by a priest. Jesus just asked us to remember him whenever we eat bread or drink wine. He didn't say go and find a priest and have them serve you communion. In fact, he was pretty critical of the priests of his time," I continued.

"If Jesus was critical of priests, I sure agree with him," Devi said.

"I have been thinking about our priests, and I just don't think that sleeping with young girls, sleeping with different women every night, and sending us out to get money and rob drug stores is very 'religious.' I like what Jesus was teaching much better."

"I will serve you communion, Devi, but first convince me that you now know who Jesus really is and tell me why you feel it is important to do something in remembrance of him."

"How about if I tell you that I don't ever want to go back to that commune? I don't ever want to worship Satan again, and if my mother doesn't feel the same way, I don't want to live with her," Devi answered.

I was shocked. Was this the same Devi?

No, I don't think so. I think this is a new Devi.

"Devi, I hope that you are serious, and I hope that your mother doesn't go back either.

"I don't know yet who this Jesus is, but I know that I like what he tried to teach us much more than I like what our 'priests' have been teaching us."

I gave Devi communion that evening, and as she finished, she bowed her head and prayed to herself. It was the first time Nancy or I had seen her pray on her own.

When Devi finished her prayer, she looked at Nancy and me and said, "For the first time in my life, I am starting to feel free. Free from Satan. Free from that coven. Free."

As Nancy and I walked back down the hallway, there was not a word exchanged. We were both in stunned silence.

On our next visit, Devi said that her mother was again coming to visit her on Saturday and asked if I would meet her at the jail and serve communion to her mother.

"Devi, I would love to give communion to your mother, but I don't feel comfortable doing so until I can meet and talk with her. Is that ok?"

Her mother's visit came, and there was no further mention of giving her mother communion, but Devi did tell us that her mother had again commented on the changes she was seeing in Devi.

The subject of Devi's mother never came up again until one evening several months later when Devi told us that I would not have to serve her mother her first communion. She told us that her mother had been going to a church in Daytona and that the pastor had given her communion.

Apparently, because of the changes she saw in Devi, her mother had been sneaking out of the coven and attending a church somewhere in Daytona.

Devi got into the advanced GED program that the jail offered and got her high school diploma with honors. She was now reading at about a high school level and had her own Bible, which she had read and underlined heavily.

Each week she would come to us with questions about what she had been reading.

When the day came for Devi's release, her mother came to pick her up. They invited Nancy and me to meet them in the parking

85

lot. They were excited to begin a new life and had plans to move out of state and away from their coven friends. They couldn't wait to begin searching for a church that they would like to attend together and swore that drugs were behind them.

As they drove off, a tear rolled down my cheek. Would they relapse, or would they stay healthy? Would I ever see them again?

"Nancy, this is way beyond anything we have done. If this isn't the hand of God and the work of the Holy Spirit, then I have never seen the hand of God or the Holy Spirit", I said as they drove off.

Chapter 18
THE DAY BEGINS

Samantha was tossing and turning on a warm August morning. She wondered how she had slipped back into using heroin after her last stint in the county jail. She had been incarcerated for several months, had completed her GED, and seemed to be doing very well when she was released.

She had worked with Nancy and me almost every week, and she had left the jail with high hopes of maintaining her sobriety and beginning a new relationship with her boyfriend, Chuck, who had been sober for over a year.

But now, it was a hot, muggy August morning several months after her release. The summer mosquitoes were huge and vicious. Samantha swatted at her arm as she felt another pinch. "Son of a bitch, is that fucking thing inside my sleeve?"

It sure didn't seem like things were going well for Samantha.

Samantha and Chuck were living in an abandoned mobile home located in a fifty-year-old waterfront RV community. The community had once been featured on postcards for Seaside Beach, Florida, but now it was only a distant memory of those golden years.

The property had been purchased by a developer, and all that remained on the property were derelict trailers that no longer had owners and were in such terrible shape that they couldn't be moved. They would all soon be scrapped, and the land would be cleared for the construction of luxury winter residences for northern snowbirds.

Samantha couldn't find any work. She was learning the hard lesson that employers were reluctant to hire ex-addicts, particularly if they had a felony record. There were a million excuses. Our liquor license won't allow it, our insurance company won't allow it, or I would love to give you a chance, but my partners won't allow it.

The harsh reality was that very few employers were willing to take what they considered to be the risk of having a druggie or a felon on their payroll.

Chuck had been working but injured his back on a construction job and was recuperating ever so slowly.

Without work, they had moved into the woods north of Seaside Beach.

After several months in the woods, someone told them about the old mobile homes, and they happily moved into one. As humble as their abando was, it was a whole lot better than living in the woods. Even without most of its windows and with no utilities or electricity, it was home to them. The living room floor was rotted, so they scavenged a sheet of plywood to lay down and covered it with a rug they had picked out of the weekly garbage. Nothing in the kitchen worked, but that was no problem. They got by on fast food and the evening meals provided by Can We Help and the churches around Seaside Beach.

They put a bucket in the bathroom with a toilet seat they had found in the Home Depot dumpster, and Chuck emptied it every day across the street in the Indian River Lagoon. Samantha hated the thought that they were polluting the waterway, but Chuck did not share her concerns.

"Hell, a little shit from us isn't going to make a damn bit of difference with what's coming out of that nuclear plant or the Indian River Plantation sewerage disposal plant. Besides that, you got a better suggestion?"

They originally thought that this would be home for a month or two, but the environmentalists were delaying the project with protests about the impact on the Indian River Lagoon, and it looked like they may have a home for a year or so.

"If we are going to be here a while, can't you get this place fixed up a little?" Samantha constantly asked Chuck.

"And oh, those damn mosquitoes. Can't you at least get some screens to put over those windows?"

"Wait a minute, that's way too big to be a mosquito. What the hell? That ain't no mosquito!" Samantha shouted as she took another swat at her arm.

Despite her best intentions, Samantha had fallen back into heroin while they were in the woods.

Samantha pulled up the long sleeve of the tee shirt that she always wore to hide her track marks, and there it was… a needle still stuck in her arm with an empty syringe.

"What the hell? What did I shoot? When did I shoot it?"

Like most nights—and even most days—last night and yesterday were a blur that Samantha could only vaguely remember through the haze of her addiction.

"Chuck, Chuck, where the hell are you?"

Chuck was not there.

"Where the hell has he gone now?" Samantha angrily shouted.

Then she heard the sound of the noisy muffler on the 15-year-old van as it pulled up on the gravel outside the trailer.

About time he got here, Samantha thought, even though she had no idea of the time or how long Chuck had been gone.

"Where the hell have you been?" Samantha shouted as Chuck came in the door.

"Relax, honey. I knew you were going to be in trouble this morning after that hard hit you had last night."

"I left to find the man and get a bag for you," Chuck tried to explain to an agitated Samantha.

"Last night, we didn't have enough money for dinner, so where the hell did you get the money?"

"I got the money, and I got your bag," Chuck answered. "Don't ask where or how."

"Don't ask where or how" was Chuck's way of saying he had probably snatched a purse off a chair back in a local restaurant or smashed a car window parked at Walmart or a supermarket to get a purse left lying on the seat. It never ceased to amaze Chuck how women would leave their purses hanging on the back of a chair while they went to the ladies' room or leave them lying in the front seat of their car while they were in a store. Snatching those purses was like taking candy from a baby.

"You better get it into yourself before you fall out. This one is going to be a hard fall."

Samantha retrieved the syringe she had taken from her arm,

checked it as best she could, and prepared for her first hit of the day. She took Chuck's bag and mixed the white powder with water in a large serving spoon.

She lit a wooden match to heat the mixture and drew it into the syringe. She didn't have anything to use as a tourniquet, so she pulled off her string bikini undies from under her long-sleeve tee shirt and tied them around her arm. In went the syringe, and in went the nectar that would prevent her from going into convulsions and the unfathomable torment of withdrawal for at least the next three to four hours.

For now, this day had begun just as every day began, getting the first hit and making plans to get the next one.

This day would be like every other. A revolving door of finding ways to come up with $100 every three to four hours to get the next bag… and the next bag… and the next bag so Samantha could repeat the process and ward off the unthinkable pain of withdrawal.

Thank God Chuck was sober, or they would have to come up with a double supply. Every day Samantha promised herself that she would get sober and they could start to make a *real* life with marriage, kids, and maybe even a house.

Chapter 19
TAKING CARE OF THE DOPE MAN

Samantha could no longer remember most of the things she did during the day, but her built-in clock made her remember the dope man's time frame.

If she couldn't get her next hit before she crashed, the dope sickness would begin.

The last time that happened, the EMTs arrived with the Narcan just in time. Without a hit or an injection of Narcan, the withdrawal was pure hell and gave her enough motivation to do whatever it took to get the next hit... and the next... and the next.

As always, she shouted, "Where are you, Chuck? I'm coming down, and you better get me a hit, or you are going to have one sick bitch on your hands!"

"Why don't you get your ass out there and get some legitimate work so you can help a little bit with the money," Chuck shouted back.

"Work? Yeah, good idea," Samantha said with a tone of sarcastic anger. "Just what the hell do you think I've been trying to do, and who do you think is going to hire someone with my record?"

Samantha had pleaded guilty to Possession with Intent to Distribute under a plea bargain that kept her out of jail but gave her a felony record. One more conviction and it would be *three strikes,* and she would have to do hard time.

Samantha's *work,* which she had mastered well, was either turning tricks on Sand Island with anyone in her black book of johns or breaking into empty condos on the island.

The locks on the sliding doors of the condos were easy to pick, and half the time, the slider wasn't even locked. Not many condos had alarms, and even if they did, it would take the police a good twenty minutes to get out to the island. By then, she would be long gone.

The condo associations made it easy to see which condos were empty. They numbered every parking slot with the condo number—God forbid that an owner may have to park somewhere other than their own parking slot. So, easy pickings, dress like a cleaning person, carry a plastic carrier with cleaning supplies, walk through the garage, make a list of empty parking slots, and start going from empty condo to empty condo.

Pills were the perfect find. From the amount of painkillers they had in their medicine cabinets, Samantha often thought that these folks must be some sick motherfuckers. However, silverware, jewelry, or anything else she could sell at the sleazy pawn shops up and down the Treasure Coast also made for a good day.

The drug man didn't give credit and wouldn't wait. Unless Samantha was standing ready with a handful of money, he was on to the next customer—no cash, no drugs. It was just that simple.

"Get me my book, and I'll call that old dude over on the island. He is always good for at least a blow job," Samantha called out to Chuck.

"I will, I will," Chuck grumbled. "But you have to get your shit organized. You are going to get caught doing these break-ins, and you can't give enough quick blow jobs to keep yourself high."

"Hook up with Ashlee and get her to put you to work over in

Golden Gate."

The Golden Gate area of Seaside Beach was once an artist colony but now was home to primarily Hispanics. The men who were here illegally and sending their money back to their home country to support their families were easy prey.

The men loved white girls, particularly blondes. As a result, Samantha, a good-looking white girl with long blond hair, would have plenty of opportunities for prostitution in Hispanic neighborhoods.

The men were paid in cash every Friday, and the girls could party with several men, sometimes turning six to eight individual tricks or gang-banging the entire house. They could steal "bonus dollars" from the men after they got them drunk. Since the men were usually illegals, they weren't about to go to the police. But don't get caught, girl. Those men imposed their own justice on the offending girls by administering severe beatings or raping them long enough and in a variety of ways until they felt they had gotten their money back.

Ashlee was a contact for the girls who wanted such work, and Samantha had been meaning to contact her to get back on the party list. One hard Friday night of work could set her up with enough money for the dope man for a week.

But Ashlee and another girl had just been busted for robbing one of the Hispanic men at knifepoint and were now in the county jail.

Samantha had heard about an older lady and her daughter who were down around Hobe Sound or Juno Beach and were running an organized prostitution ring on Tinder. But, no time for that now.

She'll work on that later. Right now, she needed a hit, and she needed it soon.

Chuck put Samantha in the old van, which grunted and groaned as it headed out onto the highway. *How long are they going to let me drive this wreck with that muffler belching out smoke and noise every time I accelerate?* he thought to himself. But with Samantha's escalating addiction and need for more and more dope, rehabbing the van was not a priority.

Where the hell am I going to get her a quick couple of hundred? The truck stop on 95? Maybe she can work the lot and get some quick cash.

As they pulled into the Pilot truck stop at Hobe Sound, it seemed like Samantha was out of the van before Chuck could even get it parked. She immediately began trolling up and down the rows until someone blinked their headlights or rolled down their window.

The headlights blinked again.

She was into the truck and back into its sleeper compartment in an instant.

Chuck went in to get himself a cup of coffee, and when he came back out, Samantha was running toward the van.

"I got the old bastard for a quick $150… didn't even have to take my pants all the way off. The horn dog couldn't wait that long," Samantha said. "Let's get down to Rivera Beach before the bottom falls out on me, and oh, by the way, stop at that pawn shop on the way."

"For what?" Chuck asked.

"For this," Samantha said as she waved an iPad she had copped from the truck driver.

"You're going to get yourself arrested if you keep stealing from these dudes," Chuck admonished her.

"Yeah, you got a better way to make money? I can only turn tricks so fast, and this is a whole lot easier on my body."

The red lights lit up on the car next to them. "Pull over shouted the officer in the passenger seat."

"For what?" Chuck shouted back.

"Just do what we just told you, and no one will get hurt. Pull over."

"I don't get it. What are we being stopped for?"

Two officers approached, one on each side of the van, with their guns drawn.

Whoa, what the hell is going on?

The officer who approached the driver's side spoke first. "If you are going to steal an iPad, why the hell would you steal the driver's iPad with his driving log on it? Are you two so damn stupid that you don't know that those things can be tracked to their exact location by GPS?"

"I'm going to read you both your rights. She is under arrest for prostitution and robbery, and you are coming in for being an accessory to both. Got it now, big boy?"

An hour later, Samantha found herself lying on a bare metal bed in the Anderson County Jail in the first stages of what was going to be a brutal withdrawal.

Chapter 20
SAMANTHA'S DAY AFTER

It had been a week since Samantha had stolen the truck driver's iPad, and I felt certain that she had detoxed enough that I could pay her a visit.

"How are you feeling, girl?"

"I'm okay, but I ain't no thief. That was my iPad!"

"Let's get real, Samantha. That iPad was the driver's log. It is GPS tracked. They can tell where it is located, how long it has been there, and how it got there. The security cameras at the truck stop show you getting into the truck, leaving the truck, and getting into your van."

"Then they tracked the iPad, and it took them exactly to where you and Chuck were found, which was coincidentally only a couple of blocks from a pawn shop."

"The good news is that the trucker is married with a couple of kids. He lives in Nevada, and I'm betting that he does not want to come back to Florida and testify as to how he took a hooker into his truck and then got rolled by her," I told her.

"As soon as they give you medical clearance, your mom is going to put her house up as security for your bail. When the trucker doesn't come back to testify, they'll drop the charges to just prostitution. You have a good family up north. Your mom is supporting you, so how about it? Are you ready to straighten up and accept the help they are offering?"

"They don't give a shit about me. All they care about is my sister, Miss Goodie Two-Shoes, her two kids, and my superstar brother, who throws a touchdown pass for them every weekend."

"That's not true, Sam. I have been in touch with them, and they are willing to get you into a private rehab if you're ready for it."

"No way. It will just be more of their damn judgment. Call Chuck and ask him to pick me up when they let me go."

"I'm one step ahead of you. Chuck was released on his own recognizance, and I went by the trailer to talk to him. He's gone. No clothes in the trailer, no sign of the van, no Chuck. Gone! Now what? Can I get back to your parents and make arrangements to get you back home to them?"

After a lot more arguing and negotiating, I finally got her to agree that I could contact her parents.

"Good call, girl. Let's see what they say."

Samantha's dad answered the phone and immediately agreed to send her money for a bus ticket.

"No, no. Can't someone come down and pick her up? You don't send an addict cash and a bus ticket and think she is going to get home safely. It's too big of a risk. She'll be off the bus and gone as soon as she hooks up with a guy or sees a liquor store at one of the stops."

"Both her mother and I work, and her siblings either have kids to take care of or are in school. So, it is a bus or nothing." Samantha's dad replied to my concerns.

Bad idea, bad priorities, I thought, but there was nothing I could do about it.

Within a few days, the ticket and $100 cash arrived.

Samantha's mother and father signed the bail bond, and she was released.

I picked Samantha up at the jail and took her to a local motel. Tom, the homeless man who was paying it forward, agreed to pick her up in the morning and take her to the bus station.

I was not comfortable leaving Samantha in the motel, but there was no other alternative. The halfway houses were all full, and so were all the shelters.

"Not a problem, Bob," Tom offered. "I'll park my van outside her door and sleep in it, no biggie. I am a very light sleeper, and if she leaves that motel, I'll know about it."

The next morning Sam headed to the bus station with Tom.

Two weeks later, Samantha's dad called to tell me that Sam had gotten home safely and had gone to rehab. But, she checked herself out after a few days and apparently took off with another patient, a male. The last anyone saw them was on a nighttime surveillance video at a convenience store they had just broken into and robbed.

They hadn't seen her since.

What could I say?

"I am so sorry. Know that you tried."

"Thank you, but I have to confess that sometimes her mother and I wish that God would just take her home, and then we would know that our poor troubled Samantha was at peace."

"Well, thank you so much for updating me, and if she shows up down here, I will let you know."

"Damn these drugs!" Bob shouted as he got off the phone.

Another young woman and her family were in chaos.

Good Lord, when are we going to get our heads around this problem and give it more than lip service?

Chapter 21
HOUSE CALL

The call came into Can We Help on a particularly busy day.

"Can We Help, how can we help you?"

A female voice said, "I'm in Ohio, but I have a winter home in Palm City. Do you have someone who could go out and check it for me?"

Most snowbirds or part-time residents had people to check on the vacant homes, but Can We Help did not offer that service.

At the same time, the other line began ringing, and a young lady with two toddlers walked in the door.

I, somewhat abruptly, told the lady from Ohio that I had another call and people coming into the office but that Can We Help didn't check people's homes.

"Here is the name of a local couple who have a business of checking homes. Give them a call," and I hung up.

Soon the office calmed down. Several volunteers had arrived, and things were under control.

I had a moment to catch my breath and felt the urge to call the woman from Ohio back to apologize for being a bit short with her. I would offer to make a call to the couple to see if they had time to add her to the list of homes they monitored.

I checked my recent call log and found what I thought was the lady's number.

But wait, that's not from Ohio. That is a local area code.

101

Maybe she has a local cell phone number since she has a home here.

I dialed the number, and the woman seemed very grateful that I had returned her call. She said that all she needed was just someone to go over to the home to check it out—she suspected that her daughter might be in the home and in some kind of trouble. She did not want to call either her homeowners association or the police to check the home before she knew more.

The woman went on to explain that she had a daughter that had just been released from an inpatient rehab facility and that they had decided that she should go to the Palm City home to rest and pursue her sobriety.

Bad choice. You don't send a newly recovering addict out on their own with their only support system 1,000 miles away.

The lady went on to explain that her marriage to the girl's father had ended in divorce as a result of the stress of the daughter's addiction and that her new husband would not allow the daughter back into their home.

The woman admitted that sending her daughter to Florida was a bad idea but felt that it was her only alternative.

Okay, don't be so judgmental, Bob. The bad idea was just a 'no other alternative' decision by a desperate parent.

The lady was concerned because she had not been able to contact her daughter for the last three days. I promised her that I would drive by the house in about an hour and would report back to her.

An hour later, I drove up to the gate of the upscale gated

community in a very nice section of Palm City. I handed the gate guard my card and explained why I was there.

"Go on through, and we don't know what you are about to find. We have had several neighbors complaining about what has been going on in there. Every time we check the complaints out, it never seems that anyone is home, and the place is quiet. But something is going on. The neighbors aren't making this up."

The house sat on a beautiful tree-lined street and backed up to a large pond. When I arrived at the house, there was loud music coming from the house. The front door was standing wide open.

Certainly much different than what the gate guard had reported—someone was clearly home, and the place was not quiet.

I approached the house calling out the name the lady had given him.

"Elizabeth, are you in there?"

No answer.

The front door was wide open, and I looked into the living room, which I could see was in complete disarray. Food containers and uneaten food were strewn everywhere, clothing was thrown in heaps around the room, a lamp was knocked over, and there was a distinct odor of filth, stale beer, and rotting food.

Sprawled on the couch was what seemed to be a woman who was either asleep or passed out – *or, wait, was that just a pile of women's clothing, blankets, and a hat sitting on the back of the couch?*

A man with no shirt or shoes and a pair of shorts looking like they were soaked with urine was sitting on the floor.

"Who the hell are you?" the man called out.

"My name is Bob, and the owner of this home asked me to come to check on it, so I guess the better question is, who are you?"

"I own this place, and I want you to get the hell out of here," the man responded.

I could clearly see that the man was in no condition to be reasoned with, so I turned and walked back out to the street. I called the owner and reported what he had seen.

The lady had no idea who the man was but assumed it was another of her daughter's "boyfriends de jour."

"I should never have allowed her to return to that area, but I thought she was serious about her recovery this time."

Being serious about recovery and actually being able to implement it are two entirely different things, I thought.

"Ma'am, could you turn down that music in the background so I can hear you a little better?" I asked.

Did that sound like the same music that I heard blaring from the house?"

"They are in there together. The place is a mess, and your daughter seems to be passed out on the living room sofa, but I really didn't get a very good look at her. What do you want me to do?"

"Please call the police," she replied. "I didn't want to have to do that, but it sounds like that is our only choice."

"I agree."

The police arrived but were reluctant to enter the home without the owner's permission. It took about a half hour for me to get the woman back on the phone, have her talk to the police, and get her to authorize the police to enter her home.

The officers instructed me to stay back and said that they would handle it from there. They proceeded to the house and returned in about fifteen minutes.

"We don't know who you saw in there, but there is no one in there now. However, you are right… the place is an absolute mess. You better get that lady back on the phone and have her get someone in there to clean the place up. If we go in again, who knows what we are going to find? If we find drugs or drug paraphernalia, we will have to file charges against someone. Probably the homeowner."

I called the owner and reported what the police had found.

She asked me if I would stay there a while to see if her daughter returned. While I was on the phone, a female officer had gone around to the rear of the property, returned, and reported that it appeared that the two people had gone out an upstairs bedroom window, jumped down onto the first-floor roof over the kitchen area and jumped off that roof onto the ground and ran.

The lady told me that she had some jewelry in a jewelry box in the bedroom and asked if someone would check to see if it was still there. The officers allowed me to go into the house to check for the jewelry box. I made my way up to the bedroom, and there it was, upside down and empty.

The police took the box, took a statement from me, wrote a report, and gave me their cards and cell phone numbers. "Call us if they return, now we have a burglary, and we can detain them if they come back."

I found a bench near the pond with a direct view of the house and decided that I would stay for an hour or so to see if anyone returned. Within a half hour, the daughter appeared, swaying and staggering toward me with a brown paper bag in her hand.

The guy was not with her.

When she saw me, she ran straight to the house. She quickly slammed and locked the door and would not respond as I rang the bell and knocked.

I called the officers, who returned within minutes. They banged on the door and announced themselves loudly enough that several neighbors came out to see what was happening.

One of the officers said, "We have a burglary suspect in fresh pursuit, and that is enough justification for me to go in."

He stepped back, then lunged forward, hit the door with his shoulder, and it swung open. He went in and came back out almost immediately.

"Get the EMTs here and make it STAT. She is out cold in the middle of the floor. She looks pretty blue and is breathing very shallowly."

The EMTs arrived within minutes and soon had the comatose lady strapped on a litter and placed into an ambulance. They began administering Narcan to combat what appeared to be a drug overdose.

In a few minutes, the lady stirred, raised her head off the pillow, and asked, "Where the hell am I?"

One of the EMTs approached me and the officers and asked, "Who found this mess?"

The officers turned to me and said, "This man right here."

"Well, if you hadn't found her when you did, we would be packing her into a body bag, not onto a litter. She was on the verge of going so far under that we would not have been able to bring her back even with Narcan."

"We've got her stabilized, and they will pump her stomach at the hospital. They will keep her overnight and then take her over to the county jail. She should be okay after a few days, but she wouldn't have made it if we were fifteen minutes later in getting here."

The next morning I checked the hospital.

"No patient by that name. She had discharged herself last night," the floor nurse told me.

"She's a burglary suspect. Wasn't there a hold on her?"

"Well, a little late for that now," the nurse responded. "She came up to the floor from the ER, and there is no notation on her chart about any pending charges."

I called the purported mother in Ohio. The call rolled straight to voicemail, and despite several follow-up calls, I received no callback. I called the number several times over the next few days, but no answer.

I checked with the homeowners association to confirm that I had the correct contact information for the owner and was surprised to learn that the home was not owned by a lady, nor was the owner from Ohio. It was owned by a single elderly gentleman from New Jersey.

I called the man in New Jersey and surprised him with the news about his home.

"Yes, I own the home. No, I don't have a daughter, and no one was authorized to be in the home."

Are you kidding me? What was actually going on, and who made that call?

Did the girl herself make the call trying to escape from her boyfriend?

What about the local area code? The police said they had tried to trace it, but it was a burner phone that couldn't be traced.

What about the music I heard in the background of the lady's call?

As I drove away, I said to myself, "Welcome to the wild and wonderful world of drugs, and no, often you will never know the real truth."

Lots of questions and no answers, but one thing was certain… someone called, and a young woman's life was saved… at least for the present.

Chapter 22
ASHLEE'S SAGA CONTINUES

"Nancy, it looks like it is going to be a busy week, thirteen new inmates over the weekend!

"But hold on there, look at this midway down the list. It's Ashlee."

"What has Miss Ashlee done this time?" Nancy asked. "I had hoped that she was doing well and was sober after her last time in jail."

"Don't know what the charges are. Just have her on the list of new inmates. We'll know soon enough, or at least will get some version of what happened, which may or may not bear some semblance to the truth."

I asked if Nancy would mind if they took Ashlee first.

"Since she is probably withdrawing, it wouldn't take long."

Nancy replied, "Of course not. You sure have a soft spot for her, but she keeps letting you down."

"I guess I do have a soft spot for her, but humor me, please."

"This time, I hope that she may finally be serious."

"You have said that plenty of times before, and I wish I shared your optimism, but I guess I just really don't. Anyway, you're the 'boss,' so let's get up there to see her", Nancy said.

"No, Nance, you know that I am not the boss. He is the boss. And I have a feeling that He has something He wants us to share with Ashlee this morning."

109

We checked in, and as we walked down that long hallway to the women's cell block, we joined hands and took turns praying about what we should say to Ashlee.

"Lord, give me the discernment and wisdom to help Ashlee this time," I prayed.

We pushed the buzzer, and a raspy *'Yes'* came through the speaker. "It's Chaplains Bob and Nancy to see Ashlee."

"Man, I'm glad to see you guys. I'm going to send her right up," the officer replied. "She has been a problem since she got here Friday night. We have to either calm her down or move her to isolation and out of contact with her or co-defendant before there is a real problem between them."

We settled into seats at a table in the conference room, and a few minutes later, Ashlee came through the door. She didn't seem to be in withdrawal, but she was in a rage. Her face was beet red. She was shouting, not speaking, and she immediately began giving orders.

"Get me out of here. Call my mother. Have her post my bail. If I have to stay here with that bitch, I'm going to kill her!" Ashlee virtually screamed.

"Whoa, girl, slow down. We can't get you out of here, and we can't relay any message to your mother or anyone on the outside. You know the drill, put your mother on your visitors' list, then I can call her and ask her to come visit you. When she gets here, you can ask her whatever you want."

"She's on my list. Just call her," Ashlee shouted.

"Okay, okay, girl, but first, why don't you calm down? Let's

110

talk about why you are here and what we can do for you."

She began a long and convoluted story about how she had done nothing wrong. She had just tried to help a friend and got jammed up in the middle of something.

No addict ever does anything wrong. They can always find someone else to blame for their problems, I thought to myself.

Ashlee went on to say that she had been sober since she had gotten out of jail the last time but that she needed rent money, so she had charged another girl to drive her to a party in Golden Gate. She said that she had only driven Diane to the house and then waited outside in the van.

According to Ashlee, Diane spent an hour or so entertaining the men, got high on some coke, pulled a knife on one of the guys, and robbed him of a sizable wad of cash.

What she saw next was Diane running out the door, screaming that someone was smacking her around, and she jumped into the van. They took off, and the next thing Ashlee knew, the flashing red and blue lights came on. They were pulled over, and they were both put under arrest for armed robbery.

Could it be that Ashlee was just in the wrong place at the wrong time this time?

I looked down at Ashlee's arms and, to my dismay, saw what appeared to be fresh track marks. She had been shooting up and had not been sober as she had told us. I did not mention the track marks and instead gave her the opportunity to just tell us her version of things.

I agreed to call Ashlee's mother and ask her to come visit

Ashlee. I knew Ashlee's mother and had very little confidence that she either would or could post the bail.

If anyone would post her bail, it was not likely to be her mother but rather her sister, who may have been the only non-addict in her family.

The next day, Ashlee's sister called me and said she was working on getting the bail money. She asked me to meet her outside the county jail next Monday.

Monday came, and I met Ashlee's sister as promised. She told me that she had written her sister off because of her repeated relapses and lies. But, this time, she believed that Ashlee was sincere and that since she and her husband were newly committed Christians, they would take Ashlee into their home one last time. I visited Ashlee several times over the next few weeks and was puzzled why her sister had not posted the bail. Then suddenly and without advance warning, Ashlee was gone.

"Gone? What do you mean? I asked the officer.

"She made bail and is gone," the officer said. "As I understand it, her sister couldn't come up with the bail money. Apparently, her mother got a bondsman to accept her dilapidated trailer as collateral. One of the conditions of her bail is that Ashlee lives with her mother, so I'm guessing that's where you can find her. "

My first thought was, *oh my God! That poor girl has no chance of succeeding in staying sober in her mother's house.*

I heard nothing from Ashlee for about two months, and the next I heard about her was when her name appeared on the list of newly admitted inmates on a Monday morning. Ashlee was back in jail, this time facing not only her original armed robbery charges but

112

additional charges for violating the conditions of her bond and new possession charges.

The two months hadn't been kind to Ashlee. She had relapsed badly, fallen hard. She didn't elaborate, but I got the impression that child protective services had stepped in and taken her daughter from her and placed her in foster care.

Ashlee looked horrible. Emaciated, tired, and, this time, clearly detoxing.

"I really fucked up this time," were Ashlee's first words when I went to visit her.

"We'll talk in a few days when you are feeling better and have collected your thoughts. But yes, this time, you really have a problem, girl."

Chapter 23
ASHLEE STARTS THE LONG ROAD HOME

Ashlee had a tough detox and did not want to see Nancy or me for a week or so. The officers reported that she was still angry and continued to blame everyone but herself for her latest relapse.

According to them, Ashlee could not cope with the fact Child Services was now involved in her life and that she might lose her daughter. She was now facing what could be several years of hard time in the Florida State Prison system on armed robbery charges.

Nancy and I knew that there was no sense trying to reason with her until she leveled out. Finally, Ashlee sent word that she wanted to see us.

As soon as they finished with Danielle, we asked the officer to send Ashlee up.

"I'm glad she finally asked to see you guys. She's been having a really tough time," the officer responded.

When Ashlee came into the visitors' room, we barely recognized her. She had lost considerable weight, her sparkling eyes were recessed and dull, and her golden blond hair was stringy and unkempt.

"I need you guys," were her first words. "They say you have to hit bottom before you can really recover, and I think I may have just bounced off that fucking bottom."

Ashlee confirmed that Child Services was involved and went on to say that no one—not her boyfriend or her mother, no one—had been to visit her and tell her what was going on with her daughter.

"This time, I am really in trouble," Ashlee said. "That girl robbed those guys at knifepoint, and I know she is going to try to spin it all onto me to get herself a sweet plea deal. But, honest to God, I was outside in the car. They want me more than they want her, and they are going to give her a 'get out of jail free' pass to roll over on me."

Ashlee's world revolves around herself. Of course, she would think that she was the most important person on law enforcement's radar.

What Ashlee didn't know was that Nancy and I had also been seeing Diane, and rolling over on Ashlee was the last thing on Diane's mind. Diane knew that she had to confront her own shortcomings and could not lay it all off on Ashlee or anyone else.

Diane had been offered five years in state prison, which meant that with time served and time off for good behavior, she would be out in about two and a half years. Diane believed that it would take her two and a half years to get her GED, get the counseling she needed, and learn how to stay sober. She was about ready to plead guilty and get the process started.

Ashlee's paranoia that Diane would roll over on her was simply a figment of her imagination.

"That may or may not be the case, girl, but don't you think we should focus on you, working on your own sobriety and getting you back in touch with the Lord? Or have you given up on God?"

My comments were followed with an addict's typical long list of *wanna-dos*—I want to do this, I want to do that—none of which were realistic. Then there was the long list of people who were going to ride in on their white horse and save her—her mother, her sister, her 'baby daddy,' her current boyfriend, and her Public Defender.

Time for a little tough love.

"Girl, you have been up and down that road for several years, and none of that has happened or worked. What's different this time?"

"None of those people have even been in to see you, much less offered any help. Your 'baby daddy' is nowhere to be found, so how is he going to be of any help with Child Services?

After offering some resistance and with some more prodding, Ashlee finally broke down and said the words that I had been waiting to hear.

"It hurts that no one will help me, but you are right... I have to do this on my own, and I can only do it with God's help."

"That's a great start, Ashlee, so let's stop with all this 'it wasn't me' stuff and accept the fact that you have done all of this to yourself. No one can fix this for you... you have to do it on your own."

"Where do I start?" she asked.

"Start with understanding that you must be honest with God. He knows your every thought, He knows exactly what you have done, He knows what you are going through, and He knows why you are here."

"You've been 'tap dancing' with God and think that you can manipulate him like you manipulate people."

"I've told you before, you can fool me, but you can't fool

God."

"He has a plan for your life, and I don't think being a doper or sitting here in an orange suit is His plan for you."

"I hope His plan includes getting me out of this shithole as soon as possible," Ashlee replied.

"To do what?" I asked.

"Where are you going to live, how are you going to support yourself, and what makes you think you won't be right back to getting high the moment you walk out the door? Isn't that what has happened every time in the past?"

"Okay, okay. What should I do?"

"How about you get down on your knees right now and give it up to God."

"Can't I do it sitting here?"

"You can, but why don't you kneel and humble yourself before God?"

Ashlee knelt and, contrary to the county jail's rules, Nancy and I laid our hands on her head. I prayed first.

"Okay, Ash, your turn."

As Ashlee prayed, "Lord, I am a mess. I have tried and tried, and I can't stop being what I am. I need you more than I need the air I breathe. I can't do this without you. Can you… will you forgive me?"

When Ashlee finished her prayer, they all stood, again violating the jail's rules, and exchanged hugs.

As they left the visiting area, Nancy and I looked at each other.

"What just happened in there?" I asked.

"He's got this," Nancy replied.

"We just need to stop talking and start listening. We don't have to do anything… just come in to see her and let the Holy Spirit do the rest."

Early one morning, several days later, I got a call from Nancy's daughter.

"Bob, Mom had a stroke last evening. She is in the St. Lucie hospital, and it doesn't look good. Can you come up?"

My knees buckled, and I lost my breath.

"I'll be there immediately."

When I walked into Nancy's room, it was obvious that she had suffered a major stroke. She was unresponsive. Her daughter said that they were keeping her alive until her son could get there from Maine.

I went to Nancy's bedside, took her hand, and prayed that God would take her peacefully and without further suffering. "I love you, and I will miss you," I whispered in her ear.

As clearly as if Nancy had actually said it, I heard the words, "I am not going away. I'll be there when you need me."

Nancy passed peacefully and without ever regaining consciousness.

The next time I visited Ashlee, I told her about Nancy and told her, "You have your own angel now. Nancy is not going to let you down."

Ashlee has been released from jail, and she is a survivor. With the help of God, and maybe Nancy, she has forged ahead.

She remains sober, is living a productive life, and is a good mother.

Chapter 24
JUAN HITCHHIKES AWAY FROM DOPE

Addiction's ugly head came to us from many directions in addition to our work in the jail.

Juan was a homeless man who had been living in Seaside Beach for several years.

Juan was well-liked by almost everyone at the evening meals and had built up a very nice business detailing cars and boats.

Juan's connection with Seaside Beach began several years earlier when he escaped a life of drugs and addiction in West Texas.

On a hot summer day, he had walked through the ten-foot cyclone fence capped with razor wire surrounding a Texas State Penitentiary. The harsh West Texas summer sun had the temperatures approaching 100 degrees, and the humidity seemed close to 100%.

He had a baggy pair of pants, a faded tee shirt, a pair of sneakers, a bag of toiletries, and $121.00 from his commissary account. That meager nest egg was all that he had to try to begin to build a new life.

Juan had just completed eleven-and-a-half years of a fourteen-year sentence for drug trafficking. He was from a Tex-Mex family that ran a cartel on both sides of the border and controlled the drug trade coming across that section of the border.

Juan was arrested fifteen years earlier when he had just turned 20.

On the day that he had been arrested, he was driving a battered pickup truck that had been fabricated by the cartel to look like a typical day laborer's truck. The truck had been carefully outfitted with a concealed rubber bladder in the gas tank. On that day, Juan had 25 pounds of cocaine with a street value of almost $1 million concealed in the rubber bladder.

Unfortunately, Juan himself had become addicted to the cocaine that he had been trafficking since he was 12-13 years old. On that fateful day, he was under the influence of cocaine and carelessly drove straight through a red light coming into El Paso.

When the officer pulled him over, his drug-sniffing dog went straight to the gas cap on the right rear fender and began barking.

"Damn it!' Juan said under his breath. "I take one shipment for a driver who didn't show up, and now I am in a world of shit!"

On that day, Juan was filling in as a *mule*. Mules were used by the cartels to transport drugs, and the cartels considered them expendable. They, their vehicles, and the drugs which were lost when they were apprehended were just a cost of doing business.

But Juan was a bigger prize. He was a family member of the cartel, and the authorities would soon be pressuring him to give them information about his family and its operations.

Juan knew better than to give up any information. Even inside the prison, there were cartel members who would quickly punish a snitch. Juan himself had given the order to "handle" a snitch on more than one occasion, and he knew that in prison, there was no tolerance for snitches.

He was not about to give up any of his family, and he had paid a high price for that silence with a fourteen-year sentence.

121

Now at almost age 35, he stepped out into the sun, and there was no one there to greet him. Most of his siblings and cousins had long since been killed in the business, moved on, or had forgotten about him. Even if the current operatives knew Juan, they weren't likely to accept him back with open arms and trust.

He was alone and had one thought. *I need to get as far away from West Texas and my family as possible. There is no reason for them to know where I am or if I am even alive.*

He looked both ways up and down the hot black ribbon of asphalt that seemed to be shimmering in the hot sun. He could tell from the sun that left was west and right was east.

West... no. Hell no... that takes me back to the family.

He looked east. *I don't know where that takes me, but I know it is in the opposite direction from my family, and that is where I'm going.*

While in prison, Juan developed severe anxieties and a profound paranoia about people. The prison psychiatrist was of the opinion that Juan's extreme use of cocaine had caused organic brain damage and that his anxieties and paranoia were very likely permanent. The doctor recommended medications, but Juan refused to take anything that would alter his moods, his thoughts, or his emotions—he had had enough of that with cocaine and crack. So he was left to deal with his anxieties and paranoia on his own.

He was able to hitch a few short rides into Louisiana, where he met a trucker at a truck stop. He had spent most of his cash on a new pair of jeans that actually fit, a shirt, a hat, and a pair of boots.

The trucker said, "You look like you could use a meal."

122

"That's for sure. I haven't eaten for about a day and a half," Juan replied.

The trucker bought Juan breakfast and asked him where he was going.

"If you are heading east and will give me a ride, I'm going anywhere you are going," Juan replied.

"I'm headed to a little place called Seaside Beach, Florida," the trucker said.

Juan replied, "If that's an invite, then that's where I'm going as well."

About twenty-four hours later, the trucker pulled up to a warehouse on Commerce Street in South Seaside Beach and said to Juan, "Here's your new home, good luck."

Juan quickly settled into the homeless people in the Commerce Street area but didn't necessarily want or need to make friends. His anxieties kicked in full throttle, and he immediately imagined that everyone he was meeting had a connection to his family.

They will find out where I am, so get the hell out of here and set up my own camp where I can control who is coming and going.

Juan located a perfect spot that backed up to the municipal airport. The high cyclone fence that surrounded the airport protected him from anyone coming into the rear of his camp. He carefully cut one narrow path into the area, which he could control with trip wires and warning bells. He could conceal the narrow path with brush when he wasn't at the camp.

Juan began coming to the Can We Help evening meals and clearly stood out. He always had a huge smile. He was very gregarious and intelligent, with a great work ethic.

He rode a red bicycle and always had two fishing poles in a homemade rod holder on the back of the bike.

He told great fishing stories, some of which may have even been at least partially true.

He had plenty of work detailing cars or boats. Juan would always show up at work with a clean long sleeved tee shirt to hide his jailhouse tattoos and was a perfect gentleman at the homes or docks of his customers.

But, his real passion was to find work as a fishing guide. How someone from West Texas developed such a love of deep-sea fishing was a mystery, but Juan sure had that love.

One evening at a meal, Juan looked awful. He was sick, very sick, and needed a room in a cheap motel for some rest. He asked me if he could borrow some money.

"Yes, but only after we get you some medical care to see what's going on in that chest of yours," I replied. We checked Juan into a motel and took him to Volunteers in Medicine the next morning.

The doctor at the clinic confirmed that he had a bronchial infection but did not feel he needed hospitalization. "This man has just run himself down from working too hard and needs to get a place to live where he can eat better and get a good night's sleep."

One of Can We Help's supporters was a local banker who had several boats and cars that Juan maintained. When he learned of Juan's situation, he and his family were determined to get Juan into an apartment by Christmas. They succeeded in finding a place, gathered furniture for it, and even put up a Christmas tree complete with decorations.

But not so fast. It wasn't to be.

Within a few weeks, Juan called me to say that he was moving out of the apartment. Despite my efforts to convince him to give it a little while longer, Juan's mind was made up.

"Why?" I asked.

Juan's paranoia had taken over.

"I don't want an address where my family or the cartel can find me, and I can't be around all this drug-related stuff."

There was no drug-related activity going on in the apartment complex. The banker and I had made sure that we had found Juan an apartment in a complex that was primarily for older people and was not drug-infested. But Juan's paranoia made his imagined drug activity very real in his mind.

Within a few weeks, Juan moved out of the apartment and back into the woods. He was very content to live in the woods and enjoyed a thriving business detailing cars and boats, but he still wanted to find a job as a first mate on charter or private fishing boats.

Juan was a human fishfinder. His ability to put boats over fish and fill the box with fish or raise up sailfish was uncanny. When fishing from the docks, no one could locate and catch snook any better than him.

Finally, he was able to connect with two local sports fishermen and got his long-sought job as a mate on their boats.

Juan still lives in his camp in the woods and is a happy man. He supports himself very nicely with his detailing work and his fishing boat work, and he is able to fish every day that he is not working.

"Note to self," I said as he left Juan at Sand Bar Park one evening.

Help these folks where you find them and how they want to be helped. You can't put square pegs in round holes, and Juan is a perfect example of how a person can be happy and self-sufficient on their own terms. We don't all march to the same drumbeat.

Chapter 25
THE POLE

Would the night ever end? Patty thought. The room was filled with smoke, most of the men were drunk, the catcalls were incessant, and the music droned on.

A few years ago, Patty had been identified on Walmart video surveillance stealing from cars in the parking lot and had served about a year in the county jail.

During that year, she had worked with Nancy and me but never seemed to have her heart into her recovery.

I had heard through the grapevine that after her release, she had hooked up with an old boyfriend, and the word on the street was that they were both using heroin as heavily as ever.

Patty spun around the pole, bounded to the floor, and did a split as the men seated on stools around the stage hooted to see her athletic body totally exposed to their leering, drunken eyes.

The stage was soon littered with dollar bills.

The song ended, as did her time on the pole. She sprang to her feet, yanked on her string bikini, and quickly gathered up the scattered dollar bills. She would now circulate through the crowd and convince one or more of the drunks to pay $25-50 for a lap dance in the back room. She hated the back room, but gathering up $1 bills off the dance floor wasn't going to get her the heroin she needed. Only lap dances with a drunk running his hands all over her near-naked body or giving a quick hand job would generate the money she needed for her next day of drugs.

Several years earlier, Patty had been an aspiring high school gymnast with college scouts coming to her every competition. They came with offers of full scholarships and promises of a starting varsity position as a freshman if she matriculated to their schools.

Patty had loved gymnastics since the days she was a child bouncing on the trampoline in her South Florida backyard. She had navigated through hundreds of age group competitions and was ultimately named the top female High School Gymnast of the Year in the State of Florida. Her days had been filled with stretching exercises, weight and strength training, and endless hours of practice on the apparatus. She had little time for boyfriends and rarely did anything outside her world of gymnastics.

But it will all be worth it if I can just get that scholarship. Patty dreamed of becoming a doctor, and her parents could not afford college, much less medical school, so a scholarship for gymnastics was the only road to her future as a doctor.

Midway through her senior year, Patty landed awkwardly on a vault during practice and immediately felt a sharp, searing pain in her left ankle. The team trainer suspected a partially torn tendon. After taking her into the locker room and doing a preliminary exam, he confirmed his initial opinion and told her that she could not compete again until she had medical clearance.

"No, no, this can't be," Patty shouted with tears streaming down her face. "I've only got three months until the States... can't you tape it and just give me something to ease the pain?"

"Patty, I'm not a doctor. I can't prescribe pain medication, and any taping that I know how to do is not going to support that ankle. You have got to see a good sports doctor and get an MRI."

Patty's coach didn't seem nearly as worried as the trainer and wasn't about to be deprived of having a state and maybe a national champion.

"You can't let this stop you now. Injury is a part of sports, and we'll just work through it," Coach told Patty the next day in his office. "Trainers aren't doctors, and they are way too conservative. My old roommate at the University of Florida is one of the best sports doctors in the state, and I'll get you in to see him tomorrow."

The next day Patty and her parents were on the way to Northern Florida. Patty was in the backseat with her leg up on the seat and wrapped in ice. After what seemed like hours of searing pain in her injured ankle, they arrived at a formidable office building.

Her father dropped Patty at the door, and her mother helped her into a waiting wheelchair. They wheeled her into the elevator and up to the fifth floor through a set of double glass doors and into a suite that looked like the lobby of a 5-star resort. The receptionist announced that they were waiting for Patty and quickly ushered her into an examination room. The doctor's assistant told her that she was going to be taken for some tests and would then meet with the doctor.

After what seemed like an endless series of tests and consultations with not one but several doctors, Patty was relieved to be introduced to the coach's old roommate, who was the head of the Athletic Orthopedic Department. He regaled her with stories about his Southeast Conference football career, where he boldly proclaimed that he had endured any number of pulls, tears, strains, and breaks but survived them all to earn All-American honors in his senior year.

Who cares about your damn football career? Can you just do

129

something for this ankle and get me back to competition? Patty thought to herself.

Finally, the doctor ran out of things to say about himself and his "glory days" and told Patty that she did have a slightly torn tendon that would eventually need surgery to repair. But he promised her that he could handle this and get her through the rest of the season without downtime.

"Then, after the season, we can get this thing repaired in plenty of time for you to start college in the fall. I can show the trainer how to tape this ankle, and we can manage the pain with no problem," he confidently told Patty and gave her an ample supply of "sample" pills before she left.

What the hell is OxyContin? Patty thought as she took the little plastic bags that held several pills each.

Wow! How many did he give me?

The doctor had given Patty one pill in the office, and it seemed to work miraculously. Before she got to the car, the pain was gone.

These things really work, Patty said to herself. *These are miracle drugs!*

The next morning, Patty headed off to school, anxious for the day to end so that she could get to the trainer and see how the ankle felt after he taped it according to the doctor's instructions. She took a pill right after classes ended and headed down for the taping.

"I'm not so sure about this," the trainer told Patty. "But who am I to argue with one of the best docs in the state?"

"Good as new," Patty told her coach and the trainer after landing a few vaults and going through an abbreviated floor exercise.

Now let's try the beam, the toughest apparatus on the ankles.

"Perfect!! No pain at all." The tape held the ankle as well or better than it was before the injury.

Fantastic. The season and my college dreams are saved. Or so she thought.

By 7 PM, the pain returned with a vengeance.

Not a problem. I'll just take another one of these miracle pills. I've got plenty.

The downward spiral of dependence on the Oxys had begun. Patty quickly burned through the sample pills but had no trouble getting the prescription renewed for ninety at a time at the pain clinics that dotted South Florida.

Patty could get as many prescriptions as she needed by simply going from clinic to clinic. All she needed was money. Patty had worked every summer since she was 13 and had a nice savings account that she intended to use to buy a car for college.

I can borrow a little from the account, no problem, Patty thought. Soon her account was gone, and the state championship was just a few weeks away. In her naivete, she went to a street vendor that someone had told her had plenty of Oxys and told him that she was out of money but would pay him in a few weeks from her summer earnings as a lifeguard.

"Sure, I can help," the street vendor told Patty. "But, I don't give no credit."

"Let's work this out so you won't have to pay me," he said as

131

he looked at her tanned, athletic body and long blond hair.

"I have a couple of guys who would love to spend an evening with you. You show them a good time, and I can give you whatever you need."

A good time? What did that mean? But what the hell? I need the pills, and how bad can hanging with some guys for an evening be?

The dealer's friends turned out to be mostly older men, and a good time was a night of sex.

Patty had never had sex of any kind, but she used Google to search porn sites and learn what to do and how to do it. It wasn't all that bad, and gymnastics season would soon be over. She would have the surgery, and all of this would just be a bad memory.

Patty's dependence on the pills began to grow, and she needed more and more pills to mask the pain. She began cutting school to turn several tricks a day and was skipping practices under the excuse of visiting schools or meeting with recruiters when she was actually working as a full-fledged drug whore.

It was only a matter of weeks before Patty was kicked off the team and expelled from school. Her parents were at their wit's end, and she was sick and tired of her father's daily lectures about getting her life together, so she jumped at the opportunity to move out of her parents' home and move in with her drug dealer.

As Patty needed more and more pills, the dealer had a solution: heroin.

The dealer, who was now Patty's full-time pimp, rented her a small studio apartment where she would meet the men and got her job in a local strip club, *The Den,* where she could earn big tips to fuel her growing heroin habit.

However, the dealer/pimp was taking almost all of her money, and Patty had to get away from him. She hitched a ride out to a truck stop on Route 95 and conned a trucker who was anxious to see the top of her blond hair bobbing up and down in his lap to take her north. She ended up in Seaside Beach and got a job in a crummy strip joint.

The new place wasn't *The Den,* and there weren't any big tippers. But if Patty hustled, she could make $200 a day, which was enough to get herself the dope she needed.

"I'm quitting this job and getting out of here. This is maybe my last shift," Patty promised herself as she began her trips into the back room to give lap dances. "I can make more than this advertising on Tinder and running ads on escort service sites."

Patty pondered how her life had spiraled down from wanting to go to college and become a doctor to being a homeless street addict who hustled johns wherever she could find them.

Chapter 26
WHO ARE YOU GOING TO SUE?

Patty walked out of the strip club that night and never went back.

She started soliciting men through Tinder ads. She learned how to return to the houses of the men who had hired her and steal whatever she could sell or pawn.

Predictably, it wasn't long before she was back in jail, charged with burglary. But, to her good fortune, or maybe not, the charges were dismissed. The men would not testify and admit publicly or to their wives that they got ripped off by a prostitute.

Patty reached out to Can We Help for financial assistance, and I tried to convince her to go into a long-term rehab, but she insisted that she was okay and could do it on her own this time.

Good luck, but when are these ladies ever going to realize that they can't do it on their own? I thought as I watched her leave the jail parking lot in the pickup truck of her boyfriend of the week.

She went straight to the condo of one of her regulars, who was always good for afternoon sex and $400-500. By the time she got free of him, she had a pocket full of cash and couldn't wait to get her first hit.

Patty left the Island, crossed the Point Bridge, and headed straight out to I95. Her speedometer went from 80 to 85 to 90 on the stretch of I95, and she soon turned off and wound her way onto the north end of Riviera Beach.

"Come on, come on, pick up your damn phone," Patty shouted at her phone.

On her third call, she heard an answer, "Publix parking lot in fifteen minutes," the voice said.

Patty sped to the Publix and quickly spotted the dope man's car.

"Hey girl, you want a special hit? Why don't you let me give you a little boost? A little China White will give that heroin a good boost, and you won't be running back and forth down here as often."

"What the hell is *White China?*" Patty asked. She had no idea that it was a street name for fentanyl. She also didn't know that fentanyl is one of the most deadly chemical opioids.

"It just gives a little boost to the H," the dealer answered.

"Is it safe?" Patty asked.

"Of course it is, girl. Take this pill, break it down, and add it to your H, and you'll get a high like you have never had."

Most street fentanyl is made in clandestine labs in Mexico with chemicals imported from China. The labs have no quality control, and their compounding of the insidious Chinese chemicals is hit-and-miss at best.

Legitimate fentanyl is 50-100 times more potent than morphine. It is used medically on only the most extreme and usually end-of-life patients. As little as 3 milligrams (the equivalent of 3-4 grains of table salt) can be fatal.

But to Patty, the concept of a better high that would last longer for only a $25 pill was more appealing than she could resist.

"Give me three bags of H and a couple of those pills," Patty said. She drove to the rear of the parking lot, crushed the pill, added it to her heroin, and injected it into her thigh.

Patty pushed the plunger anticipating a new high, but in a matter of seconds, she blacked out.

Later that evening, the security guards patrolling the parking lot found Patty in the car—dead.

Patty had my card in her wallet, so the police called me.

"Who is the lady with no ID and your card in her wallet, and who are you?" they asked me.

I explained who I was, what Can We Help was, and what our relationship with Patty had been.

"Can you ID the body and contact her family?" they asked.

"Sure."

After a trip to the Palm Beach County Morgue to identify Patty, I called the only number I had for her family.

Patty's father took his call and broke down into gasping sobs. After he had composed himself, anger rose up in him.

"I want to sue the bastards," he shouted into the phone.

"Sue who? Some lab in Mexico, some street dealer, who are you going to sue?" I asked.

I may suggest you sue the gymnastics coach, or the big shot sports doctor, or the pain clinics, or better yet, maybe sit down and think through your role in driving her up to Mr. Big Time Sports Doctor.

But now was not the time to express those thoughts.

After Patty's death was reported in the local papers, the rest of the story emerged. The gymnastics coach was fired for taking kickbacks from several colleges, the sports doctor was disciplined... his medical license was suspended, and several "pain clinics" were shut down.

Too little, too late for Patty, but at least some measure of justice.

Chapter 27
CALLS HOME

Peter was a man about 25 years old. He had been a heroin addict for several years, but his tall and strong body, good looks, and blond hair disguised the extent of his drug use.

Through Peter and his family, I was about to see the devastating ripple effects of addiction on the addict's family.

I knew that, in many cases, families were financially ruined by the costs of trying to support the addict and provide rehab. I knew that marriages of the addict's parents often break up. I saw the most vulnerable family members—often elderly and gullible grandparents—exploited by the addicts. I saw siblings who had been humiliated and bullied turn their backs on the addict.

Delaney, in her poem, said…

"…I remember thinking my family would be better off without me…"

I thought that I understood how the emotions of the addict's family often ranged from hope to anger to disappointment to abject frustration to rage, and for many, they had no choice other than to cut ties with the addict.

However, I was about to see and experience the pain of an addict's family at a level that I hadn't seen before.

Peter's sentence for shoplifting was coming to an end. Where would he go? Without a place to stay and without a job, he had virtually no chance to stay sober. If an addict returned to the environment where he lived while using and reestablished contact with friends he had while he was using, his recovery efforts were doomed.

Peter had no money or source of income, so he asked me to contact his father, who was a farmer in Ohio. He told me that he had been writing to his father and that this time his father would help him.

Peter felt that if he went back to the family farm, he would be isolated from users and dealers and could continue his recovery.

Calls to an addict's family were usually to convey bad news or to make difficult requests. They were never easy. But I made the call and had the door slammed shut immediately without any room for further discussion.

Peter's father relayed another version of a story that I had heard many times.

He said that he had put a mortgage on the farm to fund Peter's last two stints at rehab, that Peter had not only stolen from him but from other family members who would allow him into their homes, and that he had even stolen and sold his mother's wedding ring.

Peter's younger brother had dropped out of college to come home and work on the farm in Peter's absence, and no other member of the family wanted anything further to do with Peter.

The answer was no, a resounding but heartbreaking no.

"What can I do to persuade you to give Peter another chance?" I asked.

"Nothing. He created the problem. It is time for him to solve it. Thank you, but please don't call again. The Peter we knew is dead."

Dead!! The word slapped me in the face. I needed some time to digest what I had just been told. A parent had just told me that a living child was "dead" to him!

How was I going to tell Peter that his father considered him to be "dead"?

"Peter, I made the call to your father, and the results were not good," I began.

Peter shrunk into his chair and asked, "Does he know that I am serious about staying sober and that I can't do it without his help?"

"Yes, but he feels that he and the rest of the family have seen it several times before and feel that they cannot open the door again. He feels that he has to protect what's left of the family."

Peter was released a few days early and disappeared.

Since I hadn't been able to perform a miracle for him, he was angry at me and hadn't even told me that he was being released early.

A few weeks later, Peter's father contacted me and asked if he still had any contact with Peter. He said that the family had reconsidered and would take Peter back on certain conditions. I thanked the father and explained that after Peter had left the jail, I had no further contact with him. I had no idea where he was, but if I heard anything, I told his father that I would let him know that he could return home.

A few days later, one of the local police officers asked me if I had heard about Peter.

"No, but I hope he is back in jail. I need to talk to him."

"No such luck. His body was found along the railroad tracks. He was walking along the tracks and apparently never moved as the train struck him at full speed," the police officer said. "Do you know his family or have any contact information for them?"

"I do, and I will make the call. I really don't know what to say, but I'll do my best."

The sounds of Peter's father's cries of anguish told me all I needed to know about how an addict's life impacts a family.

One can only imagine the second-guessing, the regret, and the guilt that Peter's father, and many like him, will live with for the rest of his life.

Chapter 28
MARIA NEEDS THE CHAPLAIN

"They've got someone upstairs who they want you to meet with, Chaplain," the desk officer told me.

"She's a handful, but if you could spend a little time with her, it may help. She isn't from this area, and we are not even sure we have a good ID on her. She may be a gypsy. We have been having trouble with them coming into the area, and it is just about impossible to get a good ID on them. But, whatever and whoever she is, do you have time to see her?"

"For you guys, of course," I replied as she finished wanding me and pushed the buzzer to open the door to the elevator.

"Have them send her up first, and let me see what's going on with her."

A few minutes after I had entered the visiting room at the women's cell block, the door from the cell block opened. A tall, very attractive young woman walked into the room.

She could be a gypsy. She could be Hispanic. She could be Italian. Let's see who she is and what she needs.

As she sat down, I observed several tattoos on her arms, one of which caught my attention.

She introduced herself as Maria Garcia. Maria is a very common Hispanic given name, and Garcia is a very common surname, much like Smith or Jones in America. It was not uncommon that women who had entered the US illegally would use Maria, Garcia, or both as an alias.

Maria's first question to me was, "Eres un sacerdote?"

"No comprende, que is sacerdote?" I replied in my limited Spanish.

"Priest, a priest," Maria responded with a heavy Spanish accent.

My first question concerning this intriguing lady was answered. She was Hispanic, most likely Mexican.

"I am not. I am just a Volunteer Chaplain."

"Si, but can you pray with me?"

Maria said that she needed someone to pray that she would be able to escape.

"Hold on, Maria, I can't help inmates escape."

I explained to Maria that I had to report anything that an inmate said that might indicate that they intended to do violence in the cell block or were planning an escape.

"No, no yo no comprende, I need to escape from my life, not from this jail," Maria explained in a mixture of Spanish and broken English.

What was the life she wanted to escape?

I quickly skimmed her rap sheet and saw that she had been arrested for prostitution and, in fact, had a long history of prostitution and solicitation arrests. There were also several small drug and drug paraphernalia offenses, but no violence and no felonies.

Maria continued her story, saying that she had made some very bad decisions and that now her life and the lives of her children and other family members were at risk.

"If 'they' know that I want to get out, they will kill me, or they will kill one of my children," Maria said with a genuine look of fear in her eyes.

Okay, is this for real, or is this just another 'drama queen'?

Could it just be another inmate who thinks they can get themselves out of jail by creating and telling a story that they think Law Enforcement might want to hear?

Every inmate knows that Law Enforcement prowls the local jails and even plants informants who gather the information that could lead to solving other crimes. The informants are rewarded with added privileges, a lesser sentence, or even a dismissal of their charges.

"Before you tell me anything, realize that everything we are saying is being videoed and recorded. So, don't tell me anything that you don't want to have repeated or reported, " I cautioned her.

Maria took my Bible and pen and wrote a name and number on the inside front cover. "Just please call this man and tell him that I am here and that I want to speak with him."

"I can't just call random strangers and relay messages to them. That's against the rules. You need to tell me who this person is and why you want me to call him, and even then, I may have to get permission to make the call," I explained.

Maria began to tell her story.

She was married as a teenager and had three children before she turned 21. Her husband had been a violent drunk and abuser who had beaten her several times before she finally had the courage to leave him.

As Maria spoke, I looked more carefully at her tattoos. Among others, the one on her right bicep was a gothic-style cross, typical of many jailhouse tattoos. On the inside of her wrist, there were three names. I assumed they were her children's names. But the one tattoo that caught my attention was a '13' with a chain wrapped around it.

Could it be?

I had a foggy memory of hearing about the MS-13 gang and recalled that they often branded their women with a tattoo.

Did the '13' refer to the MS-13, and did the chain mean that she was bound to them?

Maria went on to say that after the divorce, she and her children went to live with her mother. Their life was just about returning to normal when she met a charming man. He not only professed his love for her but said that he wanted to become a father to her children. He drove a nice car. He said he had his own business doing motivational speaking and sales training online.

After a whirlwind few months of dating, the man asked Maria to move in with him and promised that as soon as his divorce was final, he would marry her.

Maria was smitten by this man. Her mother liked him. Her kids liked him. He seemed like a perfect match for her.

Maria was not going to pass up what seemed to be a golden opportunity for a new start for her and her children, and she happily accepted the invitation to move into his home.

The only ground rule was that the man's office was to be kept locked and off-limits to her and the children "so the kids wouldn't mess with the video and computer equipment."

After a few months, the man asked if the children could spend some time at Maria's mother's house so they could spend more time together as a couple and so that Maria could begin to meet some of his friends.

As soon as school was out, the children went to Maria's mother for the summer, and they began socializing with a very exciting group of young couples who also seemed to have plenty of money. They took weekend trips on yachts, flew to Las Vegas, and began living a lifestyle that would have been beyond Maria's wildest imagination before she met this white knight.

But as time went by, something just didn't seem to be right. Many of the women seemed to be almost robotic. They all had the same smile, and all they ever talked about was their newest Gucci bag, Rolex watch, or piece of jewelry. Maria assumed that they were just stuck-up, spoiled trophy wives or girlfriends and thought nothing of it at first.

Soon the topic of swapping partners or having group sex became a part of the conversations. When Maria balked, the man began berating her for being stiff and encouraged her to loosen up with a few drinks before they went out. The few drinks evolved into some pills and then a line of coke that would be laid out for her before they went to his friends' homes.

After several weeks, the coke escalated, and life, as she had known it, came to an end with her first injection of heroin.

"This stuff is the best," the man had said. "I won't let you get hooked on it. And if you do, we'll get you off it, no problem."

Maria's life spiraled into depths that were unimaginable to her.

It turned out that Mr. Wonderful had no online motivational speaking and sales business. He did have a business, but his business associates were, as suspected, MS-13 gang members. He was a capo, and as a capo, he was responsible for running a section of the gang's business and making weekly income quotas for the gang.

His part of the business was sex trafficking women as very high-priced escorts and pornography.

"You are going to work with me and be a part of the team, or you can just get yourself and your kids out of my house," the man had told Maria.

"If you leave, I better never hear that you have said a word about me or the others, or you and your kids will regret the day you were born."

"Is that what the '13' on your arm signifies?" I asked as Maria took a deep breath. Her left hand instinctively covered the chain and number 13 tattoo.

"Yes," she replied.

"Once he had me hooked on heroin, he could control me by controlling my supply of heroin. Because I was his biggest earner, he was not about to lose me. If the drugs didn't control me, his unimaginable violence did. He wasn't going to allow me to leave him."

Not knowing what to say next, I thought it best that I end the conversation until I could talk to someone in Law Enforcement.

"Maria, but that's all I have time for today. I'll be back in a few days."

"Bullshit!" she shouted. "You are just like the rest of them. When you hear the word MS-13, you run scared."

"All right," I said.

"You are right... I was a little hasty. So, I'm here for as long as you need to talk. But remember, all this is being recorded."

"Give it a rest. They tell you that they are recording and videoing us, but those things haven't worked for months."

And she knew that... how? Inmates know everything that happens in jail. Even things you think they shouldn't know.

Maria continued to describe her new beau's business of very sophisticated high-end escort service, video pornography, and supplying women to the disreputable strip clubs and massage parlors.

She explained that he took all of the money the women earned and provided the single ones with a crummy apartment and enough money to buy food.

"He told me I should feel lucky that I get to live in his nice house with my children, and if I didn't like it, I would find myself in one of his apartments and that there would be no room for my children."

Severe beatings became a part of Maria's life. It was like *Déjà vu* from her first marriage. But this man was not simply a raging drunk as her first husband had been. He could administer beatings with blows to the back of her head, the soles of her feet, and other places where the bruises wouldn't show. He could inflict severe pain without hardly leaving a mark.

Maria went where this man took her and did whatever the men he took her to wanted her to do. She had been gang raped, sodomized more than she could remember, and forced to record sex tapes with men and women.

She was literally owned by him and the gang.

Since he obviously knew where Maria's mother and children lived, she lived in fear that if she displeased him, he would not only take it out on her but wouldn't hesitate to harm her mother or her children.

Maria's life was a living hell until she was approached by a john, who was an undercover narc. He had taught her how to fake injecting the heroin and gave her several small vials of Narcan to use if she ever had to withdraw from the heroin.

It was the narc's name and phone number that Maria had written in my Bible.

"Please just make the call to that number I wrote in your Bible. Just call him… and the less you know, the better it is for you," Maria told me.

Suppose this is a setup with a gang member, and I walk into a trap for myself or Maria. I sure don't want this person having my phone number or being able to trace the call back to me.

As I drove home from the jail, I pulled out one of the burner phones I kept in my car's console to give to the homeless men and women and dialed the number written in my Bible. I knew that a call made from a burner could not be traced, and just in case, that burner was going to end up in the water.

149

"Who is calling?"

I was not about to give him my name and responded, "Makes no difference who I am. Maria Garcia asked me to call this number and tell whoever answered that she is in the Anderson County Jail."

Click. The call was terminated on the other end.

I drove past the turn onto A1A and proceeded to the bridge over to Sand Island. I drove to the fishing pier, walked all the way to the end, and gave the burner phone a good toss into the inland waterway.

I didn't sleep that night wondering if I had done the right thing.

Was the voice on the other end of the phone really that of an undercover police officer, or had Maria and I been tricked into telling an MS-13 gang member where to find Maria?

When I returned to the jail to visit Maria in a few days, she was gone. Discharged without a forwarding address and without bail.

Several months later, I opened the Palm Beach Post and read a lead article about a large sex trafficking and drug distribution operation that had been busted. Two sleazy strip clubs had been shut down. A large supply of drugs and weapons had been seized. A number of women who were described as sex slaves had been taken into protective custody and were expected to testify against their captors.

There was no mention of MS-13 or Maria.

But what a coincidence.

A person identifying himself as a DEA agent contacted me and asked to meet with me. The agent came to the Can We Help offices. He told me that Maria, her children, and her mother were in witness protection. He assured me that there was no record of me ever meeting with Maria at the jail and, in fact, there was no record of her ever being in jail.

After the conversation, the agent left, telling me that "this meeting never happened, and you never met with Maria."

That Christmas, I received a simple Christmas card with no return address, no signature, just a carefully printed note:

"Estamos bien. Gracias por hacer la llamada. Feliz Navidad (We are fine. Thank you for making the call. Merry Christmas)."

Chapter 29
WHY DID THEY HAVE TO DIE?

Maria's story stayed with me for a long time, and I wondered how many other young women were caught in that snare of sex trafficking. But at least Maria and her family were seemingly alive and well.

Others like Peter, Delaney, Patty, and Sue were not so fortunate. Each of them had been making strides toward their recovery, but tragically none of them could beat their addictions, and it cost them their lives.

What are we doing to help these poor people overcome the death grip of addiction?

Are we doing enough?

Are we taking this seriously?

Or are we going to pass off each death as just another 'junkie'?

Those questions haunted me, and I could not get them out of my mind.

Every day social media regales us with the tale of some celebrity, athlete, or some other person of means checking themselves into one of the famous treatment facilities.

But, those programs are far beyond the means of most addicts.

The sad fact is that there is practically nothing available to the average young addict who may be living on the streets, in abandoned dwellings, in cars, and whose families will no longer even take their calls.

Once they find themselves in jail, where do they go when they are released?

Where do they live?

Where do they find food?

How do they get transportation to outpatient treatment facilities or even to 12-Step meetings?

How do they get a job with a "record"?

All too often, when they are released from jail with a plastic bag of their personal items and no money in their pockets, their immediate challenge is to simply survive.

The natural inclination is for each addict to go back to what they knew before their incarceration. That decision almost always leads them right back into the dark world of drugs, sometimes within days, even hours.

We delude ourselves into thinking that there are halfway or sober houses available for folks coming out of jails or rehabs. Indeed, there are many facilities that carry the name halfway, safe, or sober houses, but not many are anything more than a halfway stop on the way back to active addiction.

They aren't cheap. $300-440 per week is a normal fee to rent a bunk bed in a room with four to six others and the right to sit in a living room and watch television. Each person then buys their own food and competes for room in the refrigerator and cooking time in the small kitchen with a four-burner stove.

Arguments and fights abound.

They are gold mines for unscrupulous real estate investors who

153

can multiply the rental income from a three-bedroom home to several times the rent that they could charge for a single-family home.

Too often, they are nothing more than a sophisticated version of slum lording, which is protected against zoning restrictions under the Americans with Disabilities Act.

They are easy targets for predatory drug dealers who have a captive audience of eight to ten people to whom they can easily sell their drugs.

I began addressing the issue of these so-called halfway or sober houses with anyone who listened, and as a result, I gained the reputation of being a rabble-rouser.

"Why are you causing such a problem?" I was asked by county officials.

"I'm not causing the problem. I am just addressing it," I replied.

"How can we expect men or women coming out of jail to succeed when we don't even have suitable housing, much less supportive programs, or professional help for them?"

"Look, we didn't create their problems… they did. It's up to them to fix their own problems. Maybe they should just stay away from drugs!" I was told.

All right then, problem solved! Just stay away from drugs! Are you serious? And do you have any idea what you are saying? Obviously not.

City leaders and Chambers of Commerce do not want it to be known that there are homeless people or drug addicts in their little paradises. After all, who is going to retire to their beautiful communities if we let them know that there are homeless people and drug addicts there?

"The county has to put its resources and money where it matters the most," the city's leaders told me.

"And, where would that be? Printing fancy brochures to attract tourists and retirees?" I argued.

"Go out and raise the money to build a facility," I was told.

"Suppose I did so. Would the county consider giving us a few acres out of the thousands of acres of land it owns so we could build a facility?"

"Most of that land is already spoken for. We are building a new fairground. We want to build a new visitors center, we need to expand the sewerage treatment plant, and we need more playgrounds."

I had now gone far beyond the comfort zones of the county leaders. I was now the troublemaker who was upsetting their peaceful world with all this talk of homelessness and addiction.

"How many homeless do we actually have in Martin County?" I asked the Housing Director at an Affordable Housing Committee meeting.

The answer triggered a long, rambling answer about walking through every acre of woods, using Sheriff's officers to assist, and even using helicopters to locate the homeless camps. "And," she proudly announced, "as a result of that concerted effort, we can confidently say that we have about fifty-eight homeless people in the county."

I laughed out loud.

"I'm sorry I didn't mean to be rude."

"But, last night, we served fifty homeless people meals, so are you saying that we fed all but eight of the homeless people in this entire county? Are we going to get real about this, or are we just going to turn our heads, let people die, and pat ourselves on the back with bogus statistics?"

Not surprisingly, I was not reappointed to the Affordable Housing Committee, and I suddenly found myself getting nothing but lip service from any other governmental or funding agency.

I quickly learned the meaning of the term 'NIMBY.'

Yes, we all have empathy for the problem, but *Not In My Back Yard.*

Chapter 30
THE CIRCLE IS COMPLETE?

I decided to take a little time off and think about the frustration I was feeling.

Can We Help was growing beyond being able to be run by volunteers. We needed a professional Executive Director. But before we could commit to an Executive Director, we needed reliable funding to pay the person. In order to get the funding, we needed an Executive Director to effectively submit the applications for the funding.

It was a classic chicken and egg dilemma.

I had learned that funding agencies such as the United Way and Foundations spoke their own languages and, frankly, were not user-friendly nor receptive to newcomers.

I learned that non-profits and their funding agencies were a very incestuous group. They all gave Can We Help polite deference but were not about to allow a newcomer into their clique.

Even if we could get the funding for housing or a treatment facility, we would have to deal with the county officials who would be happier to see all the homeless and addicted people simply disappear from the county rather than create programs to assist them.

Their jobs and their re-elections were dependent upon stimulating a vibrant tourist and retirement industry, and anything that interfered with that was inimical to their own self-interests.

Could we continue, or had they done all that we could for the homeless and addicted community and had to pass the torch to someone or something else?

It was a beautiful sunny day in South Florida, and I had decided to spend the day on my patio, watching the golfers go by and contemplating the future of Can We Help.

I should have played today... but, nah, I think I will just sit back and think.

Just then, my cell phone vibrated on the table, and I saw an out-of-state number that I didn't recognize. *Spam again*, I thought, but for some reason, I reached down and answered.

"Do you know who this is?" said the clear voice of a young woman.

"No, but if it is Medicare or an extended warranty for my car, please just lose my number," I sarcastically answered.

"You knew me as Devi. Do you remember that name?"

Devi!! I hadn't heard from her since that tear rolled down my cheek in the parking lot as she and her mother drove off from the jail.

Was she okay? Had she relapsed? How did she even get this number?

"My mom had this old cell number, and we were hoping that it still worked."

"It is so great to hear from you. How are you and your mother doing?" I asked while holding my breath to hear what I expected may be a request for money or a sad story of relapse.

Devi went on to say that she and her mother had moved to a small town in Iowa where they had some cousins. Their cousins had encouraged them to come to Iowa, telling them there were practically no drugs, certainly no Satan worshipers, and that it would be a safe environment for them.

"Well, that was a year ago tomorrow, and a lot has happened in that year," Devi told me.

Still waiting for the other shoe to drop, I waited for Devi to say, "...and we just need a little money to help us over the hump." That was usually where these conversations went.

"I officially changed my name... no more Devi... no more Devilia. I am now Deborah. I chose the name Deborah because Deborah was a female in the Old Testament who helped her people overcome impossible problems. It reminds me that Mom and I need to continue to overcome our own problems and to help others to do the same."

Could this be the same Devi who didn't even know who Jesus was and spent her entire early life worshiping Satan?

"Mom and I are both sober now and love it here in Iowa. We have found a great group of women, and Mom is actually leading a women's Bible study for AA women. She is really enjoying sharing her transformation with others and encouraging them to follow her lead."

I took a deep breath to regain my composure.

Mom, the devil worshiper, was leading a Bible study! Who said miracles don't happen anymore?

"We opened a little shop where we sell products that local women make. Knitting products, quilts, jams and jellies, candles, and home-baked bread, cookies, and cakes. We don't make a lot

159

of money, but it is enough for us to support ourselves and is a great outlet for some of these women's products."

"I have met a wonderful guy and think I may get married in about six months, but only if we can work out a way to have a mother-in-law apartment because I won't leave mom alone.

"And, are you ready for this… I cook meals once a week for some homeless and really poor folks who come to the church for a once-a-week dinner. Me!! Cooking!! Can you imagine?

"As our one year of sobriety rolled around, we wanted to reach out to you, thank you, and give you the good news."

"Devi, sorry, Deborah… that is just the news I needed today. I was sitting here feeling sorry for myself… a couple of overdose deaths have really hit me hard. Thanks so much for sharing your good news with me."

"Mom and I laugh all the time about how stupid we thought it was when you first began telling us about Jesus casting out demons and all that stuff, but now we are proof positive of what He can do if you will only let Him."

"Deborah, you give your mother a big hug, and I will hang on to this for a long time. Thank you, thank you, thank you?"

Chapter 31
STRENGTH IN NUMBERS

After my conversation with Deborah, I had a renewed enthusiasm to try to continue the work of Can We Help, even though it was obvious that we could not do it without help.

Perhaps we can establish partnerships with other community non-profits and share resources. We may not all need individual grant writers or executive directors, and perhaps, we can be far more efficient by combining efforts and sharing resources.

I began contacting other organizations in the community that served the jail, worked with the homeless, or reached out to the addicts. Several organizations were interested enough to at least come to an initial meeting.

The early meetings taught me some harsh realities.

I learned that many organizations weren't about to give up what they considered to be their alpha dog role in the community.

I learned that a faith-based organization wasn't taken seriously by most of the funding agencies, and they would often deny us funding because "it wasn't legal" (which is completely inaccurate, but nonetheless a convenient way for them to say no).

I learned that the homeless and addicts were not appealing candidates for most funding agencies. It was much easier for them to focus on Vets, single moms, abandoned animals, green projects, or other warm and fuzzy causes.

I felt like Don Quixote, tilting with windmills!

Although some of the smaller groups liked the idea and wanted to cooperate, the larger groups were very resistant.

The larger groups had been doing the same things over and over for years and were convinced that they had it figured out. They were content to continue doing things that made themselves and their donors feel very proud but which produced very little boots-on-the-ground results.

It seemed—but it wasn't then nor is now up to me to say—that the larger organizations were primarily motivated to maintain their bloated staffs and large salaries.

Every organization could recite its own list of statistics and perceived accomplishments, but not many had ever actually looked directly into the eyes of those who needed help. Not many had ever gone into the woods to actually meet and talk with the homeless. Not many had held an addict's hand as the life ebbed from their bodies.

At one meeting, I talked about the recent overdose deaths. To my dismay and amazement, a representative of one of the organizations actually said, "What can we do about addiction? We've learned that we are just throwing money away until these addicts decide they want to get sober."

Oh my God, why don't we just ask the blind to see, the lame to run, and the mentally ill to think more clearly? Then we can deal with them on our terms and not get our hands dirty dealing with them on their terms.

"If we think we are all doing a good job, why is the problem getting worse instead of better? Why are people continuing to die? Why is the relapse rate so high if what we have been doing is the answer?" I asked as a rhetorical challenge to the group.

No real answers.

After several frustrating months of trying to develop a cooperative approach, I had to concede that it was a utopian goal that wasn't about to become a reality.

Is it like in other communities?

I reached out to other communities across Florida and even outside the state, and the answer became apparent—it is the same in most other communities. Stay in your own lane, don't rock the boat, and above all, don't criticize the status quo.

In the course of my search, I made contact with an extraordinary program in Tampa, Florida. Metropolitan Ministries had not only developed an extraordinary program but were willing and anxious to share their experiences and expertise with others.

Let's arrange a day trip for Can We Help people and any other non-profits that would like to join us, and maybe we can learn something from Metropolitan Ministries.

Metropolitan Ministries readily agreed to allow the group to spend a day at their facility in Tampa and to offer the group whatever assistance they could from their years of developing and operating a highly successful program. They could accommodate up to ten and would set up a full day of touring their facility and meeting with their operating personnel.

I invited representatives of ten Seaside Beach non-profits to join me for a day in Tampa. The result: one organization agreed to participate.

The negative responses...

"We have checked them out, and they aren't doing anything

we don't already know about."

"They are faith-based, and we have moved away from that."

"Folks, this is a proven program that has a success rate of getting about 85% of the people that they contact out of homelessness and addiction and into jobs and housing. They have been extraordinarily successful in helping addicts get sober and reintegrate into society. Isn't it worth a day of time to check them out?" I pleaded.

The responses he received were, "Maybe next time" and "Thanks for thinking of us."

Next time, I'm not sure there is going to be a next time.

Chapter 32

THE DOGS BARK, and THE CARAVAN ROLLS ON

After several futile months of attempting to get adequate financing, build community partnerships, and learn from other programs across the state and across the country, the Board of Can We Help had to face the reality that we could not continue.

 There was much more that needed to be done with the homeless and the addicted, but without staffing and without funding, we could not attempt to address the multiplicity of needs.

 With enormous remorse, the office that had been provided to us through the generosity of a local church was closed.

The church itself took over the primary responsibility of preparing the weekly meals, and the loyal volunteers who had been serving those meals continued in the same capacity.

The jail ministry was reduced and focused only on female inmates who were addicts.

The programs to assist single mothers who needed resources, support, and training had to be abandoned.

The clothing and food bank was delegated to other community thrift stores and food banks.

The life skills and vocational training programs that had been conducted at the offices had to be terminated.

 As disappointing as all of that may have been, we all had a sense of pride. Pride in knowing that we had done all that we were capable of doing to help the "least of these my brothers and sisters."

An old friend had once used the phrase: "The dogs bark, and the caravan rolls on." It now seemed very appropriate.

The *dog* of drug addiction continued to bark... and bark increasingly loudly as an unconscionable number of our youth died.

But the *caravan* rolled on.

The *dog* of homelessness continued to bark... and bark increasingly loudly as our streets and parks continued to fill with homeless encampments.

But the *caravan* rolled on.

The *dog* of politics continued to bark.

But the *caravan* rolled on.

The *caravan* of finger-pointing—let's blame the other party, let's blame the other candidate, but wait, who is blaming the cartels, the warlords of Mexico, or the state-owned Chinese facilities that are making the chemicals that become fentanyl?

The *caravan* of funding agencies will not fund faith-based organizations and judge the effectiveness of their funding on the basis of the number of people impacted, not by the effectiveness of the programs.

It was a sad day as I, Sandra, and the other volunteers cleared out Can We Help offices and wound it down.

"You look like your mind is a million miles away," Sandra said to me.

"No, not a million miles away. Just pondering Matthew 25: *'Truly, I tell you that whatever you didn't do for the least of my brothers and sisters, you did not do for me.'*

"Did we do enough?"

Chapter 33
THE MIRACLE OF DALE: THE BLIND CAN SEE

Ironically, as Can We Help began to wind down, a columnist from the Seaside Beach News, Eve, contacted me and asked if she could write an article about the dinners for the homeless.

"Of course, we would be honored, and it would go a long way toward getting new volunteers to assist the church in continuing the meals," I replied while telling her what was happening with Can We Help.

"But, please, no pictures of the homeless and no names. Many of these folks do not want to be identified, and we want to respect their privacy."

"No problem, we will only photograph the volunteers and the guests if they allow it."

The designated Thursday evening arrived, and the reporter arrived just as scheduled. Several of the homeless guests were surprisingly willing to speak with her, and one of them, a man named Dale, even agreed to have his picture taken and published.

The next day's edition of the paper had a front-page article with a color picture of Dale sitting on the ground with his back against a tree, eating his meal.

My cell phone rang.

"This is Diane at Volunteers in Medicine. What a great article. Let me ask you something. Is Dale's sight impaired?"

"I don't think so. Why do you ask?" I asked.

"Just the way he looks in the picture. I could be wrong, but ask him, and if it is something as simple as glasses or cataracts, we will take care of it for him."

I knew where Dale lived and tracked him down. I asked Dale if he had any problem with his eyesight, and to my surprise, Dale responded that he couldn't even make out my face. He explained that he had moved his camp so that he didn't have to cross any highways to get where he needed to go and that he had even given up riding his bicycle.

"Would you like us to see if we can get that taken care of for you?"

"Sure as hell. What can you do?" Dale replied without hesitation.

"I'll arrange to take you up to Volunteers in Medicine, and let's see what they can do."

The scheduled day to meet Dale came, and Dale was a *no-show*. Several more dates were set up, but again, *no-shows by Dale.* Finally, I gave up and assumed that Dale had changed his mind and didn't want the help. There were often reasons why the homeless didn't want help or didn't want to be identified, so I simply let it pass.

Several months later, my cell phone rang.

"Bob, this is Dale."

"Dale, where are you?"

"I'm sitting here in the woods. Where the hell do you think I am– at the Ritz Carlton?"

Thinking that Dale needed some food, a blanket, or whatever,

I asked him what I could do for him.

"Does that offer to have my eyes looked at still stand?"

"You bet it does, but what changed your mind?"

Dale explained that he hadn't thought that he could stop drinking and was afraid that the doctors wouldn't operate on him if he was drunk or had alcohol in his system. But now, he had finally decided to sober up and have his eyes looked at.

"I am either going to be a dead, blind drunk out here in the woods, or I am going to accept the help you people are offering."

"Here's the deal," Dale said. "I am going to a VA thirty-day rehab, and I'll call you thirty days after I get out. If I have stayed sober for those thirty days, I hope that you will trust me."

"I will absolutely trust you and will be waiting for your call. Yes, I will help you."

After his rehab and the thirty days, the doctors decided that Dale's loss of sight was the result of long-standing, untreated cataracts. They were optimistic, but not certain, that they could surgically remove his cataracts and, hopefully, could at least restore some sight.

At Dale's one-week post-operative check-up, the results were miraculous—100% success. His eyesight was a perfect 20/20.

By that time, Dale had been sober for about three months and was adamant that alcohol was in his past. No more drinking, and now he just had to find a job and a place to live.

A friend of his from AA ran a legitimate Christian-based sober living house and offered Dale a free room in exchange for doing cleanup and maintenance work. He would also have to set up and run two AA meetings a week at the house.

Done deal, perfect for Dale.

Several weeks later, the golf pro at our club said that he needed someone to do odd jobs around the club and asked if anyone knew of someone who wouldn't mind starting at the bottom with a chance to progress.

In full transparency, I explained Dale's background and circumstances, and the pro and the Board agreed to give him a chance.

Dale was thrilled. He could bicycle to the club from his apartment at the sober home and loved the opportunity.

But would folks accept him?

"That's up to you," I told Dale. "Do your job, do it well, just be Dale, and I'm guessing that you will be pleasantly surprised at how much people are willing to accept you."

Over the next several months, Dale became a "rock star." He not only did great work at the club, but he picked up many odd jobs from the members. He was soon making more money than he had made in years.

Dale contacted and reconciled with his twin sisters. He was so proud the day that they were able to come visit him and even prouder that he had saved enough money to pay their expenses. Their reunion was magical, and Dale was as proud as a peacock showing them around the golf club in "his" golf cart. He entertained them with a dolphin cruise and rebuilt a relationship that had been lost in a vodka bottle for twenty years or more.

Chapter 34
WHAT DO YOU MEAN HE DIDN'T SHOW UP?

"Bob, have you heard from Dale?" It was the golf pro on the other end of the phone. "He didn't show up at work today."

My heart sank. *Had Dale relapsed? It couldn't be. He was doing so well.*

"I don't have a clue, Dean, but I'll try to track him down and let you know."

That doesn't sound like Dale. I sure hope all is well.

Expecting the worst, I went to all the old places and people where Dale used to hang out. None of the guys had seen him.

"Haven't seen him since he left the woods and moved to his apartment?"

I went to Dale's apartment and banged on the door. No answer. I walked around and saw no one else on the property. Just as I was leaving, the owner pulled up.

"Have you seen Dale?"

"No, I am just getting here. Have you tried his apartment?"

As we walked down to Dale's apartment, the owner flipped through a ring of several keys. "I think this is Dale's."

As we opened the door and stepped in, we were both stunned. Dale was lying on the bed in a pool of blood.

"Oh my God, what happened here?"

I dialed 911 as the owner checked Dale.

"The good news is that he is still breathing and seems to be alive."

The ambulance arrived within several minutes and quickly loaded Dale.

"We need to get some blood and fluids into him, or we are going to lose him. Follow us to the emergency room if you wish, but stay out of our way until we can assess what has happened here."

Within minutes, they had Dale connected to several IVs and were off with sirens blaring and tires spinning in the gravel driveway.

I sped to the hospital and sat for what seemed to be hours. I called Dale's sisters and told them what we had found.

"I have no idea what happened. It looked like he may have been shot or stabbed, but I really don't know, and they haven't told me anything."

"Call us as soon as you know anything, and we will try to make arrangements to get down there."

"Are you here with Dale?" the nurse asked.

"Yes, is he okay?"

"They've moved him up to ICU, and the doctor has asked that you meet him up there."

As I entered the ICU, the doctor came out immediately. "Your friend is in bad shape," were his first words.

"He is in acute liver failure. He woke up long enough to tell us that he thought he had indigestion, so he took several Alka Seltzers throughout the night. Couldn't have done anything much worse. There's a lot of aspirin in that stuff, and it only exacerbated the bleeding. I think we can stabilize him, but the extent of the bleeding tells us that he has serious, if not end-stage, cirrhosis. The damage may be more than he can survive. If he has any relatives, I would suggest you get them here."

"Dorothy, the prognosis is not good. Apparently, it is liver failure. I didn't know that liver failure could cause such hemorrhaging, but it sure can. The doc suggests that you guys get here ASAP."

"We can get a flight into Palm Beach, arriving at about eight. Can you have someone pick us up since we don't know the area, and it will be dark?"

"Someone will be there for you. Look for someone holding a sign in the baggage claim area with 'Dale' on it."

I went in and sat down next to Dale, who was in a deep sleep.

After a lifetime of extreme alcohol abuse, it seemed that Dale's liver had simply given out. His age and history as an alcoholic contraindicated that he would be a viable transplant candidate, so the prognosis seemed bleak.

At about 9:30, Dale's sisters arrived. By that time, the doctors had been in and out of the ICU many times, and with each visit, the prognosis became worse.

"He will be lucky to make it through the night," the doctor told them.

Dale's sisters and I stayed with Dale, sang to him, prayed for him, and held his hand as he turned more jaundiced and his breathing became very shallow. He finally passed away without ever regaining consciousness.

"We expected the worst and talked about this on the flight down. We would like to have him cremated and have a small service down here. All his friends are down here now. Then we want to take his ashes back home and bury him. His parents will be so happy to have their son back home."

"I didn't know your parents were still alive."

"Oh, they are not, but they will know that he is back home with them."

Chapter 35
I GET PAID

Dale's death impacted a wide circle of people.

His homeless friends saw him as an inspiration. The golf club members loved his upbeat attitude, his great smile, and his work ethic. His family rejoiced that they had been reunited with him, if only for a year. His sisters made arrangements to stay in Seaside Beach for several days so that there could be a small memorial service to celebrate his life.

One of Can We Help's former Board Members was an ordained minister who offered to conduct the service. I persuaded a local funeral home to offer their facilities for a small service.

"We don't expect more than twenty to twenty-five people," I told the funeral home. My estimate was grossly incorrect. Over a hundred people came to the service. Many wanted to speak about how Dale had influenced their lives, how Dale had given them hope to improve themselves, and what a pleasure it was to have known the new Dale.

One of Dale's sisters spoke and brought tears to everyone's eyes when she thanked everyone who had a hand in giving their brother back to them, even if only for a year. She spoke of how they would have always wondered what had happened to their brother if they had not been reconciled with him and expressed great comfort in knowing that he would be back home lying at rest next to his mother and father.

As she spoke, my thoughts drifted to the others who had died.

What could I have done? What could the system have done to

176

give those families the same wonderful feelings of peace and relief that Dale's sister was expressing? Maybe nothing. Maybe Dale was just a singular miracle.

After the service, Sandra and I stayed with the sisters until all the guests had left. Dale's sister, Dorothy, came up to shake my hand, and I felt something in her hand.

Was she giving me money?

"Dorothy, you don't owe me anything. I did what I did for Dale because he was a good man."

"No, no, you deserve to have this, and please keep it to remember our brother by."

I looked down, and it was Dale's One Year of Sobriety medal from AA.

"I can't take this. Please, give it to a family member or keep it yourself."

"No, it's yours. You gave us our Dale back, and I want you to always remember him and remember what you did for him and our family."

That small piece of worthless metal was worth more to me than any money I had ever earned. It is now the most important piece of jewelry in our home.

I read the inscription on one side: *To thy own self be true,* and on the other: *God give me the serenity to accept the things I cannot change. Courage to change the things I can and the wisdom to know the difference.*

"Dorothy, you have no idea how much this means to me."

177

Dale, speaking through that small medal, gave me the serenity to accept the things that I could not change and the confidence to know that I had been true to my own self.

But, above all, *to his own self, Dale had been true.*

Chapter 36
AN UNEXPECTED CONTACT

After Sandra and I closed Can We Help, we decided to leave South Florida and relocate to South Carolina.

Was it compassion fatigue?

Was it simply the need for a change?

Was it just the Lord leading us in another direction?

I really didn't know, but we moved to South Carolina.

A few years later, I was updating my Facebook and contacts when a friend request popped up.

Danielle wants to be your friend.

Danielle!!!

I hadn't seen or heard from Danielle since that night almost five years ago when she told me that she was being released from jail the next day. I responded immediately and scrolled through my contacts to see if I still had a telephone number for her.

"Honey, you won't believe this," I said to Sandra. "I just got a friend request from Danielle. Do you remember her?"

"Sure I do. She and Ashlee were two of your favorites when you were doing the jail visits."

"I have no idea if this old cell number is still active, but I am going to try to call her."

"Success!"

Danielle answered on the first ring. "Could this be THE

Danielle that I knew in Florida?" I asked.

"The one and only," she replied.

"My God, girl, what a treat to hear from you. What have you been doing?"

"Long story, Bob, but since I saw you last, I have had my ups and downs and did some time in state prison. But now I am sober, and things are really going well."

"I am living in the Keys and have met a wonderful lady that is my life partner. After all, I had been through with prostitution and all, I just couldn't make a meaningful relationship with a man."

"It is so wonderful to hear from you and even better to hear that things are going well. I have actually been thinking about you, Ashlee, and a number of the women from the days at the jail because I am trying to write a book about all of you."

"That should be some story," Danielle replied. "What is the book about?"

"I want the readers to get to know each and every one of you and to see the horribleness of drug addiction and homelessness on a personal level.

I want the reader to see your faces just as I saw them.

I want the reader to know who you are, how you are hurting, and how you struggle.

I want the book to show people that drug addiction and homelessness are not just words… that you are real people who live, struggle, die, and sometimes succeed. Will you help me, and do you still have contact with any of the women that I could reach

180

out to?"

"I want to help you, and yes, I can put you in contact with Ashlee and a few others."

"Ashlee, oh my gosh. How is she doing?"

"She is out, sober, and still a devoted mother to her beautiful daughter."

"And you?"

"For right now, we are here in the Keys, but I am going to take a job as a counselor at a Christian rehab facility in Nebraska, and we will be moving out there soon."

"Danielle, you have given me a whole new reason to write this book. Those that are still fighting their addictions need to know that if you and Ashlee can do it, so can they."

Over the next several months, I communicated regularly with Danielle and Ashlee. Both Ashlee and Danielle have provided invaluable help for this book, and there is no better place to end the story than with the success stories of these two strong, spirit-filled, and successful young women.

They and the other survivors of these horrible plagues on society are proof positive that...

"You can do what you have to do, and sometimes you can do it even better than you think you can."

Jimmy Carter

58 poem

Ron 7

Made in the USA
Coppell, TX
12 October 2023